What's in a
West Berk
Wood?

And how did it get there?

Dick Greenaway

Dedicated to the men and women of the West Berkshire
Conservation Volunteers of the West Berkshire Countryside
Society (formerly the Pang Valley Conservation Volunteers)
who through their dedication and hard work over many years
have looked after our countryside and improved it for us all.

First published 2016

First published by West Berkshire Countryside Society.

www.westberkscountryside.org.uk

2016

ISBN 978-0-9543597-7-5

Book design by Rowena Coles Design

Printed and bound by ESP Colour Ltd, Swindon.

© Copyright Dick Greenaway 2016

CONTENTS

ACKNOWLEDGEMENTS

This book could not have been published without the generous support of The Bucklebury Estate, The Gerald Palmer Eling Trust and Lord Robert Iliffe of Yattendon. I would like to thank them most sincerely for their help and encouragement.

As with every author, I have been educated over the years by very many people, most of whom didn't realise they were doing it at the time! To them all I offer my thanks and I hope I haven't misinterpreted their words of wisdom. If I have, the fault is mine alone.

However, there are those that I must name and to whom I owe a great debt of gratitude for their patience and help. Nick Hopton introduced me to image manipulation (of the nicest sort) and has drawn many maps, plans and profiles without complaint. Dr Michael Keith-Lucas cast his eyes over my first chapters. My daughter Anwen took many of the woodland pictures and Sarah Orr of the West Berkshire Historic Environment Record patiently and efficiently supplied me with multitudes of local information. Over the years I have made extensive use of the Berkshire Record Office and both Newbury and Reading Local Studies Libraries. Their staffs have been unfailingly skilled and helpful.

I would particularly like to thank Yattendon Estates and their staff – particularly their gamekeepers – who have tolerated my strange requests and helped and encouraged me in my studies of their woods. Many other woodland owners have allowed me access to their woods and estate records. The records of many of the older estates are a goldmine of local history.

I must gratefully thank Rowena Coles of Rowena Coles Design for the way she has taken my drab WORD documents and patiently turned them into a vibrant and attractive book.

Finally I must thank my wife Jill for her professional archaeological advice and for her careful and painstaking editing which has made this a much better book.

The images – pictures and diagrams – are mainly from the many taken by Jill and myself over the years (The Greenaway Collection). All others are acknowledged individually. Reading Museum requires an acknowledgement that will not fit under the photograph. I have shortened it to 'Reading Museum' this should be read as 'Reading Museum (Reading Borough Council) All rights reserved'. The French Ministere de la Culture et de la Communication Centre national de préhistoire has a similar requirement and I have shortened this to 'Centre national de préhistoire'.

I have tried my best to identify the copyright owners of all the pictures I have used. If I have given a mistaken origin I offer my apologies.

Dick Greenaway
Ashampstead Common
October 2016

Geological Periods

Atlantic Period c.6,200 to c.3800BC. Fully developed 'wildwood'.
Holocene The present geological period.

English Archaeological and Historical Periods

Palaeolithic (Old Stone Age) c.500,000BC to c.10,000BC
Mesolithic (Middle Stone Age) c.10,000BC to c.4,000BC
Neolithic (New Stone Age) c.4,000BC to c.2,500BC
Bronze Age c.2,500BC to c.800BC
Iron Age c.800BC to 43AD
Roman 43AD to 5th century AD
Anglo Saxon 5th century AD to 1066
Medieval 1066 to 1485

Technical Terms

Aurochs A very large wild ox.
Bavin A tightly bound bundle of twigs used as firewood.
Bolling The stump of a pollard from which poles grow.
Copse, Coppice Woodland where the trees have been cut off near ground level and the resulting new growth harvested at regular intervals.
DNA Deoxyribonucleic acid. The coding contained in cells for making the organism. Examining the code allows the identification of plants and animals from organic remains.
Interstadial A warm period between Ice Ages.
Maiden or Standard A tree that has been neither coppiced nor pollarded and simply left to grow naturally – sometimes with a little pruning.
Pollard A tree cut off when young at about 2m–3m above ground level so that the spring (new growth) is above the reach of grazing animals.
Refugia An area where plants and animals continued to grow throughout the Ice Ages.
Spring The new shoots from a coppice stool or a pollard bolling.
Stool The tree stump resulting from coppicing.
Wildwood A fully developed and purely natural woodland cover.

I had the good fortune to be born and brought up until my mid teens in a house on the eastern edge of Oxford. If I walked out of the front door I entered a community of tarmac and brick, of beautiful buildings, of libraries and museums staffed by knowledgeable people willing to help me. If I walked out of the back door and wriggled through a hedge I entered a different community. A trot across two fields took me into Brasenose Wood with the wide open rabbit-grazed spaces of Shotover above and beyond it. I recognised from an early age that the communities were quite separate and self contained but that each could affect the other either for good or for ill.

My friends and I spent a lot of time in the wild community, playing at being explorers, playing war, building camps and climbing trees – all the things government programmes now try, with limited success, to get children to do. In my case the time gave me a great love for the wild.

At sixteen I became a sailor and learned to navigate my ship around the world using measurements of the sun and stars and I learned to record the weather and the sea. Later I became a hydrographic surveyor and made charts of the sea. Measuring and recording and drawing became an even more satisfying way of life.

In the early 1970s my wife and I came to live on the edge of 200 acres (about 90 hectares) of open mixed woodland and I indulged my love of looking and measuring by resuming my involvement with the wild community. I started studying and mapping the woodland and I recorded its plants, trees and archaeological features. It soon became apparent that these quite different elements were actually very closely linked. The use mankind had made of the land over the millennia had been constrained by the soils and the soils had also controlled the species and distribution of the trees and plants growing in the wood. These, in turn, had governed the use made of the wood and resulted in the archaeological features. Some years later I was invited to examine the woods on Yattendon Estate and a deep interest became almost an obsession!

Later still I started to be asked to give talks on my findings and it was during one of these that it occurred to me that the images I was showing and the script I was speaking had the makings of a book. The talks were generally well received and so a book might be equally well received and anyway, the 'putting it on paper' was the usual end product of a surveyor's efforts. This book is the result and at this point I must make it clear that I am an amateur in the true sense of loving the subject. I have no professional training in botany, palaeobotany or history. Be warned!

In the book, firstly I look at the effects of the last Ice Age on our countryside, then where trees and plants survived and how they eventually spread back to us and created the original 'wildwood'. In the final chapters I discuss how the woods were used by the communities around them and what relics of this use can be seen. The penultimate chapter suggests ways of 'getting to know a wood'. All the way through, plants and animals are intermingled in the story.

Most of my examples are from the Pang Valley – my special study area – but are applicable to the rest of West Berkshire. I make no apology for the number of footnotes. This is a very general book and anyone wanting to take the subject further should find them useful.

Figure 1. A veteran sweet chestnut with a story to tell.

Figure 2. In the last million years Britain has spent more time under ice than under grass and trees.

Chapter 1

A clean sweep.

You are standing in a West Berkshire wood. It is early morning in Spring. The air is still – hardly enough breeze to stir the new leaves. The low sun is shining through the branches and showing up every fold and hollow in the woodland surface. The bluebells are at their best and are starred with wood anemones. There is a complete absence of human noise. No cars, no aircraft, no loud voices. This is as it has always been in the immortal woods.

But has it? We take our woods almost for granted. We tend to assume that any wood, other than an obvious plantation, has always been there 'from time out of mind'. But has it really?

In the last million years Britain has spent much longer under ice than it has under trees and vegetation. In that time there have been eight major glaciations or Ice Ages with short warm interglacials lasting a few thousand years between them. We are currently in an interglacial that started about 12,000 years ago. The previous interglacial was the 'Ipswichian' – named for the site near Ipswich that supplied the evidence for its date and climate. It took place about 130,000 years ago and lasted for about 11,000 years[1]. During the subsequent glaciation, temperatures dropped to as low as -20°C and ice caps over modern Scotland were up to 3km thick. This is the distance from Newbury to Thatcham or from Hungerford to Froxfield – but straight up! Solid ice!

Even though the ice sheets probably did not reach West Berkshire they stopped not far to the north[2]. The landscape south of them would have been tundra, frozen to a great depth, barren and desiccated and covered with blowing sand, snow and ice fragments.

It is obvious that trees and vegetation are unlikely to have survived in such conditions. Perhaps a few tough lichens and mosses – but not trees. If you go back far enough everywhere was clear and tree free.

[1] Roberts N (1998) *The Holocene* p56

[2] Britice Modelling Project Aberystwyth University
www.aber.ac.uk/en/iges/research-groups/centre-glaciology/research-intro/britice-model/

Figure 3. Tundra.

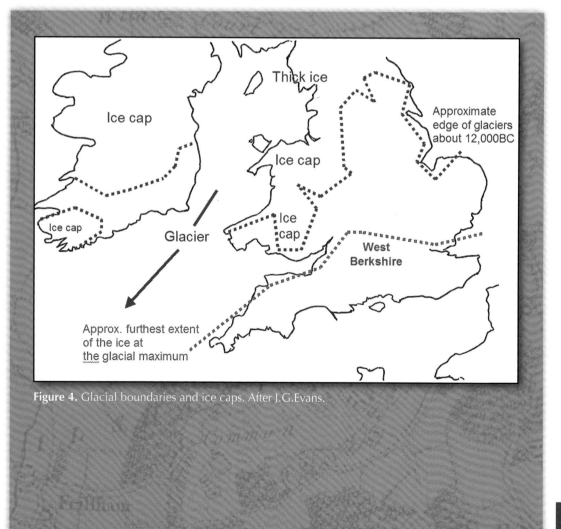

Thick ice

Ice cap

Approximate
edge of glaciers
about 12,000BC

Ice cap

Ice cap

Ice
cap

Glacier

Ice
cap

West
Berkshire

Approx. furthest extent
of the ice at
the glacial maximum

Figure 4. Glacial boundaries and ice caps. After J.G.Evans.

Survival in the *Refugia*

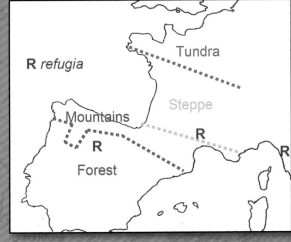

Figure 5. *Refugia*[3].

Clearly trees and plants did survive somewhere otherwise there would have been no vegetation to spread back to us. The areas where the survival took place are known as *Refugia* or 'refuges' and, as can be seen from the map (Figure 5), are clustered along the southern edge of Europe. The areas that appear to have supplied southern Britain and Ireland lay in the Iberian Peninsula, southern France, northern Italy and possibly the Balkans.

The modern landscape of the Iberian Refugia in Portugal and Spain is characterised by deeply cut, steep sided, sheltered valleys with winding steams whose flora is remarkably similar to chalkland streams. There is a particular abundance of water crowfoot. In some places one could almost be in the Lambourn valley.

It may seem strange that a plant refuge would be sited in a mountainous area but the reason is simple. Amongst mountains plants can adapt rapidly to changes of temperature by simply dying off in the higher areas when the climate cools and then expanding up the mountainside when warmth returns. The distances are short and the up-hill expansion is aided by warm air moving up a mountainside (Figures 8 and 9). Whereas in flatter areas a drop in temperature will sterilise a large area and the equivalent rise in temperature may take many generations of plants to recover the lost ground.

---

[3] Source http://www.earth4567.com/talks/ice.html

Figure 6. Flora in the Iberian *Refugia*.

Poppy

Foxglove and hawkweed

Mullein

Water crowfoot

Figure 7. The Iberian *Refugia* today.

Figure 8. Plants 400m below the crater.

Figure 9. Plants near the top of Mt. Vesuvius. The volcano last erupted in 1944. Photos taken in 2014.

What survived to spread?

There is a temptation to think only of trees when we ask 'where did our woods come from', but we should really think of entire ecosystems – communities made up of plants, trees, animals, insects, birds, amphibians and molluscs – with mankind rattling around amongst them all. They were inter-dependent – particularly the animals. The herbivores could not leave the plant-rich bubble without starving and the carnivores could not leave the herbivores. Our ancestors began moving up from Africa in around 23,000BC and there is evidence that hunting groups did move considerable distances north following the herds in summer and then returned south again in the winter[4].

Figure 10. Two aurochs, a pony and deer painted around 15,000BC. Lascaux. Centre national de préhistoire.

---

[4] Manco J. (2013) *Ancestral Journeys p53*

Figure 11 Two European bison. Lascaux. Centre national de préhistoire.

We know which animals lived in the refuges because the humans who shared them painted the animals' pictures in the caves and rock shelters where they lived. They also engraved very similar drawings of them on rock faces along the sheltering valleys. Figures 10–14 and 26, show examples of these pictures. Unfortunately, the cave and rock artists usually only depicted animals. Very few birds, plants or people are shown. Our only way of identifying the plants present in a refuge is by testing scraps of wood left by the artists deep in caves and by studying pollen that has survived in oxygen free layers of mud in swamps and lakes. Pollen for analysis comes from cores taken in deposits of ancient muds and peat, but peat bogs are rare in the warmth of the Mediterranean. However, there are a few[5] and these show that birch, oak, hazel and elm were present in SW France and that pine, birch and oak had survived in NW Spain.

So here we have a collection of plants and animals in existence and ready to spread once the climate had warmed sufficiently to allow them to.

---

[5] Bennett KD (et al) *Quaternary Refugia of north European trees* in Journal of Biogeography (1991) 18. p107

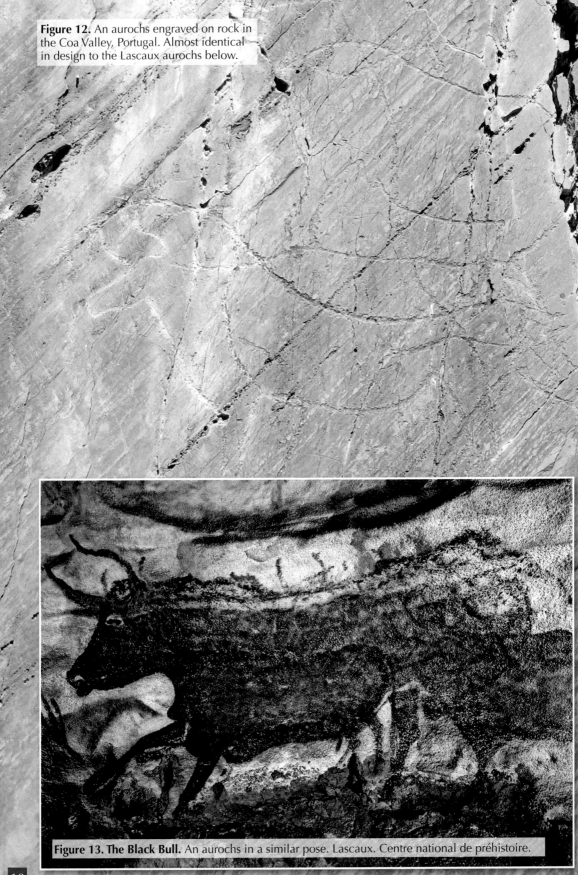

Figure 12. An aurochs engraved on rock in the Coa Valley, Portugal. Almost identical in design to the Lascaux aurochs below.

Figure 13. The Black Bull. An aurochs in a similar pose. Lascaux. Centre national de préhistoire.

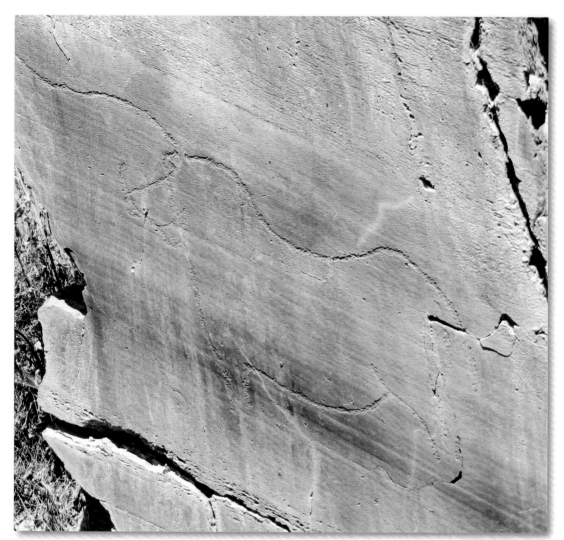

Figure 14. Pony. Coa Valley, Portugal. Compare this with the pony in the cave painting in Figure 26. The line above the head is part of another animal. Paul Bahn has suggested that these engravings date from between 8,000 – 22,000BC[6].

[6] Bahn P. (2007) *Cave Art* 231

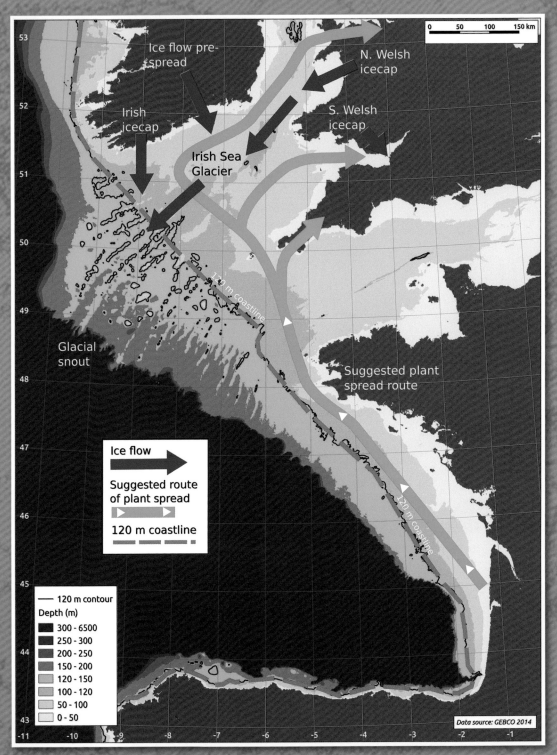

Figure 15. Suggested ecosystem spread from the Iberian and southern France *Refugia*.

Nick Hopton

Chapter 2

The spread.

For a number of very complex reasons the earth's climate warmed suddenly, starting about 18,000BC, and rose steadily with a number of lapses until the present day (Figure 16). In 18,000BC sea level was about 120m below its modern level and the coastline followed the orange pecked line on the map in Figure 15 – a long way west of the present shoreline. As a comparison, Kintbury village sits on the modern 120m above sea level contour. This provides some idea just of how much lower the sea was!

As can be seen on the profiles in Figure 18, the area between the water's edge and the rising ground of the modern coastline formed a reasonably even and slowly rising shelf running along the whole western edge of France to Ireland and Western England and Wales. This would still have been comfortably wide when the melting ice raised the sea level to 100m below the present level in about 10,000BC. It enjoyed a micro-climate warmer than the land mass to the east. This was provided by its low altitude and the relatively warm sea along its western edge combined with shelter from the cold continental interior supplied by the high land of modern France (Figure 17).

At its narrowest point off the westernmost tip of Brittany it was still nearly 100km wide and I suggest that it was along this shelf that the returning vegetation expanded towards Britain. Pollen data seems to show that hazel spread into southern England from the west rather than the south route would explain such a spread if hazel came up the Irish Sea 'valley' and around the North Welsh icecap into the Midland Plain.

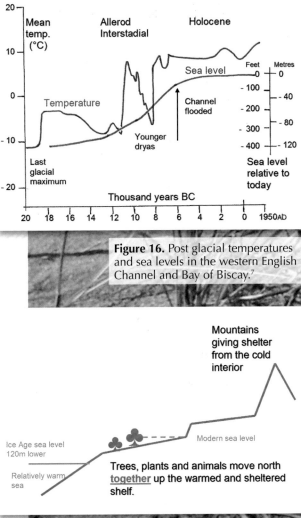

Figure 16. Post glacial temperatures and sea levels in the western English Channel and Bay of Biscay.[7]

Figure 17. Coastal shelf.

---

[7] Beebee T. British Wildlife 2014 p234
Redrawn with permission.

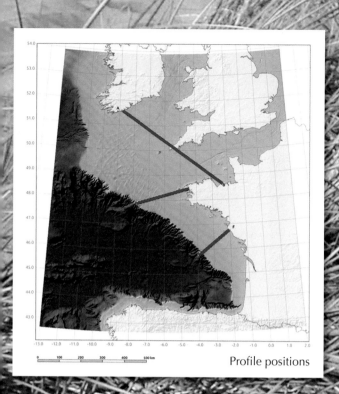

Profile positions

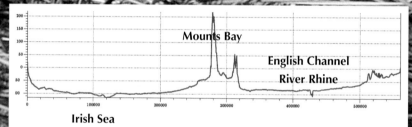

Mounts Bay

English Channel

River Rhine

Irish Sea

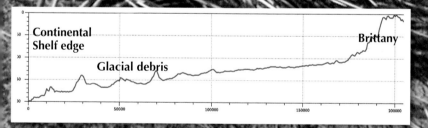

Continental
Shelf edge

Brittany

Glacial debris

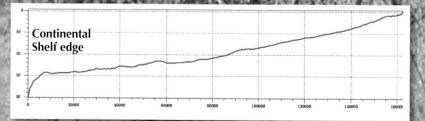

Continental
Shelf edge

Figure 18. Shelf profiles

15

There is a large and growing body of evidence that this is the route our returning woods took. Of course, any physical evidence on the shelf has long since been destroyed by the sea, but a quick look at a few of the links between the Iberian Refuge and the British Isles will be useful.

The science of DNA and the worldwide sampling of plants and animals are providing good evidence of migration routes. The spread of ash die-back disease (*Chalara fraxinea*) across Europe has stimulated the investigation of the DNA of ash trees and the results have shown that British ash trees are more closely related to Iberian ash than to central and eastern European ash. (Figure 19)[8]. Animal DNA recovered from bones found on archaeological sites reveals a link from Iberia up the west coast for brown bears, hedgehogs, pygmy shrews and red deer[9]. (Figure 20). Even slugs have a link. The only two places in the world where the Kerry slug is found are in the NW corner of Iberia and in SW Ireland[10]. And as a final touch, the collection of archaeological finds of human occupation found in Duruthy Cave in SW France has very close parallels with that found in Kendrick's Cave in North Wales.

An interesting, but totally un-scientific, link is to be found in Irish Invasion Mythology where several invading armies are given Spain as their places of origin!

Figure 19. The distribution of Ash in Europe by DNA.

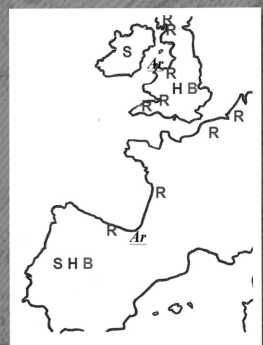

Fig.20. Brown bear, Hedgehogs, pygmy Shrews and Red deer links by DNA. *Ar* archaeological site.

[8] Pautasso M. (et al) (2013) Biological Conservation 158 37–49

[9] O'Connor & Sykes (2010) *Extinctions and Invasions* 192–3

[10] Beebee T British Wildlife April 2014 229–35

The mechanisms of the spread

It is all very well to claim a route for the spread and to provide correspondences at either end, but from the southern corner of the Bay of Biscay to the Irish coast is a thousand miles (1,600km). Can plants and small animals really spread that far? Well, yes they can. Initially the seeds of the very hardy shrub juniper (Figure 23) were carried north into the tundra by migrating birds – notably Lapland buntings. Wind blown birch seed can spread widely and the trees reach seed-bearing maturity very rapidly. (Figure 21). Anyone who has walked over Bucklebury Common will have noticed the density of the pine saplings which have spread from a small group of Scots pine trees planted by a misguided early 20th century enthusiast! Willow's roots and branches trap silt and build up organic soil with its leaf fall

Over very many years the tundra soils increased in depth and fertility and the climate warmed enough for trees to grow. Pine and birch that thrive on poor soil came first with willow and hazel close behind. Elm and oak followed soon after.

Figure 21. Dense birch woodland.

Figure 22. A muddy willow pond.

As with juniper, seed eating birds probably provided most of the original spread. For example, in a good mast year a single jay will collect several thousand acorns and will bury them up to 4km from the parent oak tree. Nuthatches and the continental nutcrackers collect hazel nuts in a similar way.

Figure 23. Juniper.

Nevertheless, pollen analysis of cores taken in southern Britain shows that it was a long time after the climate had warmed enough for deciduous trees to thrive before they actually arrived[11].

We are fortunate, in West Berkshire, to have two key pollen sites in the Kennet Valley at Woolhampton[12] and at Thatcham[13] that have provided reliable information about the very early period at the end of the Ice Age; Woolhampton, from about 18,000BC to about 8,000BC, and Thatcham from about 7,900BC to about 7,500BC. Another site near Oxford at Cothill Fen and Sidlings Copse carries on the sequence to the Late Roman period[14].

At Woolhampton juniper and willow arrived in about 10,000BC followed by birch about 300 years later. At Thatcham, by about 7,900BC birch made up 60% of the tree cover with 37% Scots pine. In the understorey there was 29% willow and 6% hazel. Four hundred years later (c.7,500BC) this had become 68% Scots pine, 26% elm, 4% birch and 2% oak. In the understorey hazel had expanded massively to 70% with 13% willow. Hazel nuts abound on Mesolithic sites and they seem to have been an important part of peoples' diet. At Thatcham broken hazel nuts were found in large quantities around the remains of hearths. Indeed, man may have helped spread hazel by favouring hazel groves and dropping ripe nuts.

At Cothill Fen and Sidlings Copse the tundra landscape with scattered Scots pine and birch gave way in about 8,000BC to hazel, elm and oak. Small leafed lime and alder arrived just before the introduction of farming in about 4,000BC and became an important part of Midland woods.

[11] Roberts N (1998) *The Holocene 99 et seq.*

[12] Collins, Fenwick, Keith-Lucas & Worsley (1996) *Late Devensian river and floodplain dynamics and related environmental change ..... at Woolhampton, Berkshire, ...* Journal of Quaternary Science 11 (5) 357–375

[13] Wymer J (1962) *Excavations at the Maglemosian Sites at Thatcham, Berkshire,* and Churchill DM (1962). *The Stratigraphy of the Mesolithic Sites III and V at Thatcham, Berkshire.* Proceedings of the Prehistoric Society Vol 28. 329–361 and 362–370.

[14] Day SP (1991) *Post-glacial vegetational history of the Oxford region* in New Phytologist Vol 119 issue 3 445–470

Figure 24. Early woodland was not dense. It was kept open by grazing animals. Windsor Great Park. Jill Butler.

Figure 25. Pasture woodland.

Chapter 3

The early woodlands and the first clearances.

The early woodlands were not dense. They covered the whole of southern England and further north apart from a few inhospitable spots and they were kept open by the populations of herbivores that had spread from the *refugia* with the rest of the ecosystem[15].

[15] Vera FWM (2000) *Grazing Ecology and Forest History*.

Mesolithic man seems to have had a limited effect on the woods[16].

The populations of animals roaming these early woodlands were controlled only by the natural agents of disease and starvation, and by hunting by man and other predators. Therefore the herds were probably very large – as were the vast herds of bison in North America and the huge herds of animals in Africa reported by early European explorers. Open areas would become overgrown if a plague struck the herds or if a particularly hard winter reduced their numbers. As the survivors multiplied other areas would be opened. A modern example is provided by the way scrub invaded open land when *myxamotosis* hit the rabbit population in the 1950s. I vividly remember the rolling acres of short rabbit-nibbled grass on my youthful playground at Shotover. Sixty years later they are completely covered with trees and bushes.

Figure 26. Aurochs cow and pony among plants. Lascaux. c.17–15,000BC Bridgeman Images.

---

[16] Roberts N. (1998) *The Holocene 194*

Figure 27. Wild boar.

We should not underestimate the ability of the herds to clear vegetation. The aurochs, for instance, was a massive beast. An aurochs bull could be 1.8m (six feet) high <u>at the shoulder</u> and had a very dangerous set of horns. Hunting by men and possibly wolves would only have had a limited effect on their numbers and a creature this size required very large volumes of both vegetation and water. They certainly lived on the Kennet floodplains where their bones have been found in the peat[17]. Wild boar[18] and beavers also lived in these areas and created wallows, beaver dams, ponds and glades. Finds of flint knapping debris in patches about a metre across where someone sat making flint tools have shown that Mesolithic people made use of these clearances[19].

---

[17] Peake H. (1931) *The archaeology of Berkshire.* 30, 31

[18] Peake H. (1931) *The archaeology of Berkshire* 13

[19] Froom R. (2012). *The Mesolithic of the Kennet Valley.* 5, 152, 214

Figure 28. Beaver.

Figure 29. Roe deer.

The woods on the higher and drier downland were probably kept open by our two native deer – red and roe. Ponies were also present in the early Mesolithic but became scarce and may have died out before being re-introduced in the Bronze Age[20]. There is no doubt that substantial trees did grow on the high chalk because root holes have been found in archaeological excavations, for instance in the excavations at Rams Hill[21]. They had gone by the Early Bronze Age when over a thousand 0.3m diameter oak trees had to brought – probably from a wood in the Vale to the north – to revet the face of the rampart of the new defended enclosure[22].

In the Mesolithic Period, between about 10,000BC and about 8,000BC, after a rise in temperature of something like 17°C in less than a century (Figure 16), a huge meltwater lake in NE Canada discharged very cold fresh water into the North Atlantic when the ice dam impounding it melted. It entered the North Atlantic via Hudson Bay at the very point where the cold water could do the most harm to the warming climate. The cold fresh water floated on top of the warmer and denser salt water and completely disrupted the ancient Gulf Stream and the North Atlantic Drift that had been warming NW Europe. The climates of a swathe of Europe from the Mediterranean to northern Britain and from Iberia to Turkey changed dramatically[23]. The eastern end became very dry but the western end became wetter and cooler. In Ireland and Britain the coolness and the wet encouraged the formation of peat bogs. In some places the water table rose, drowning the roots of trees and killing them, and their fallen trunks are sometimes found preserved in bogs. These finds would have been rare in West Berkshire because the chalk geology does not encourage bogs, but very thick layers of peat certainly built up along the Kennet Valley.

The woodlands at this time were probably as close to the concept of 'the Wildwood' as they ever have been. The Cothill Fen and Sidlings Copse cores show a mix of small-leaf lime and alder with hazel as an understorey. Oak was certainly part of the general mix and beech had come up through central France and reached the Midlands by about 2,000BC. Ash and elm were widespread but sparse. Just imagine the scent of miles of lime trees in the Spring!

---

[20] Bendry R. (2010) *The Horse* in *Extinctions and Invasions* O'Connor T and Sykes N (Eds) 10.

[21] Bradley, R. and Ellison, A. 1975, *Rams Hill: a Bronze Age defended enclosure and its landscape*, BAR 19. 206

[22] Keith-Lucas M. in *Rams Hill: a Bronze Age defended enclosure and its landscape*, BAR 19. 122

[23] Proceedings of the National Academy of Science USA 2012. 'Meltwater routing and the Younger Dryas' Codron A and Winsor P.

Figure 30. Red deer.

Neolithic man's impact seems to have been small to start with – merely the creation of garden type plots that were abandoned when their fertility declined. An analogy with Papua New Guinea is appropriate[24]. I had the great good fortune to meet Professor Paul Sillitoe of Durham University at a conference and he described to me his experiences in remote areas of Papua New Guinea in the 1970s at the time the people were converting from a Stone Age culture to a steel-using economy[25]. Our conversation began with me asking if a stone axe could <u>really</u> cut down a tree? I had handled many stone axes – both Mesolithic and Neolithic (see Figure 32) – and found it difficult to believe that they would seriously damage an oak tree, let alone fell it. He explained that the technique was different and that trees over a foot (0.3m) in diameter were regularly felled. He had timed felling with a stone axe and then the felling of a similar tree by the same men using steel axes of the same general size and had found that felling with stone took only about 1½ times as long as felling with steel. However, the usual way of making a garden plot was to cut the understorey and

[24] P.Sillitoe (1979) *The Lithic Technology of a Papua New Guinea Highland People* Dept of Sociology La Trobe University Bundoora.

[25] Sillitoe P (1979) *Stone Versus Steel* in Mankind 12 (1979) 151–61

use it to make a fence, then to girdle the larger trees and light a large fire around them. This killed the trees and removed the leaves and smaller branches, thus reducing the shade and fertilising the soil. They then farmed around the trees which eventually fell down. When the soil fertility was exhausted the plot was abandoned and a new one created. Nature moved back and within 50 years the plot was woodland again. If this procedure was used in Britain it would have produced the spread of charcoal in the soil that has convinced archaeologists that Neolithic people used 'slash and burn' techniques. However, we must remember Oliver Rackham's opinion that 'British woods burn like wet asbestos'!

Farming, both arable and pastoral, arrived in Britain from the Middle East around 4,000BC and its introduction did eventually have an impact on the woodlands of southern Britain. Flocks of newly introduced sheep added to the effect of the natural herbivores by grazing off tree and shrub seedlings. Newly introduced goats had a serious impact on the shrub layer by browsing off low-lying branches and bark.

Figure 31. Wayland's Smithy Neolithic long barrow.

In West Berkshire the high chalk area was cleared first and the excavations at Wayland's Smithy Neolithic long barrow show that it was built in open country. The chalk was tackled first, not only because the soil was lighter and better drained, but also because it probably had a thin layer of wind-blown *loess* on its surface which, when mixed with the chalk, produced a calcareous soil with a high pH very suited to growing cereals.

In the late Neolithic and during the Bronze Age the size of the population increased dramatically. The growing demand for food accelerated the rate at which the woods were cleared. Iron tools were introduced soon after 800BC and made clearing land even easier. No longer could plots be taken at will and later casually abandoned. Instead, carefully surveyed grids of fields were laid out within substantial 'ranch boundaries' – some as early as the Bronze Age. These were large banks and ditches some of which, like Grim's Ditch near

Figure 32. Neolithic axehead. Reading Museum.

Figure 33. Bronze Age palstave. Reading Museum.

Figure 34. Grim's Ditch – a probable Iron Age ranch boundary near Aldworth.

Aldworth (Figures 34 and 78), survive in West Berkshire woods. These large areas were then sub-divided into well-organised small fields like those in Figure 81 at Streatley Warren. The Streatley Warren fields were cultivated in the Bronze Age, Iron Age and Early Roman Periods and then abandoned around 200AD when the fertility declined[26]. But those banks protected from damage by Ham Wood survive in as pristine a condition as when the last Romano-British farmer left them and they are covered with a splendid collection of wild flowers. (Figure 82).

---

[26] See Chapter 6 note 54 for links.

By the start of the Roman Period it is thought that there may have been even less woodland in southern Britain than there is now[27]. Julius Caesar, gives us our first written account of southern Britain in 55 & 54BC.[28]

> *The population is exceedingly large, the ground thickly studded with homesteads and the cattle very numerous ……. there is timber of every kind, as in Gaul, except beech and fir.*

Beech charcoal has been found on much earlier archaeological sites in the Midlands and Caesar must have marched through beech on his way through Kent and Essex. The confusion has occurred because early translators translated … *except sweet chestnut* … as … *except beech*[29].

The Romans were highly organised. Their well-built and defended towns were linked by straight, purpose-built roads. Rivers were bridged rather than forded. Merchandise was paid for with centrally struck coins rather than traded by barter. All this led to centralised production rather than local and domestic production. For instance, although there were local kilns, industrial scale production of high quality pottery took place at centres such as those around Oxford, in Dorset and in the New Forest. Iron smelting was a major industry in the Kentish Weald.

The Roman administration eventually collapsed under a succession of invasions through the borders of the empire plus serious plagues and reluctance on the part of the citizens to get involved in public service. The essential services demanded by the Roman lifestyle – such as road and bridge maintenance – ceased to be carried out. The production and distribution of vital daily items – coinage, pottery and metalwork – became impossible. The skills needed for home production had withered and people were unable to replace the manufactured items. Taken together these led to a drastic decline in the standard of living and a fall in population. As a result some cultivated land reverted to woodland and major Roman sites have been found in areas known to be wooded in the Middle Ages.

---

[27] Rackham O. (2006). Woodlands. 63.

[28] Caesar J *The Gallic War* Penguin 1960 135 footnote

[29] Dr M Keith-Lucas *Pers. Comm.*

Figure 35. *'Woodland at two pigs!'* Modern pigs in woodland.

The next written sources to provide a useful quantity of information are Anglo Saxon charters. Charters are land transfer documents and give the boundaries of the land to be transferred in great detail. These descriptions frequently contain trees as boundary marks.

In 956AD King Edwig, or Eadwig, granted *a grove with its glades* at *Hafochrycg* or *Heafoc Hrycg* to Abbot Aethelwald of Abingdon Abbey to supply building material to repair the church of St Mary. Both names translate as 'Hawkridge'. I was able to relate the boundary to an area NW of Stanford Dingley where almost all of the 10th century features still exist. Sadly, although the boundary was very well described it gave no indication of the make up of the wood other than to infer that it was very open and included oaks!

However, the Anglo Saxon love of, and skill in, recording did mean that when Count William of Normandy conquered England in 1066 he inherited a skilled and educated 'civil service'. By 1086 he had destroyed the power of Saxon landowners and replaced many with his supporters. In the process many land-holdings had changed their boundaries and they had all become manors. In order to assess the payments and services he could extract from his kingdom he ordered a great survey of the manors in the country using its trained civil servants. This was carried out in a single year and was preserved because it provided proof of ownership. Some landowners preserved their pre-conquest charters as well to demonstrate the origins of their ownership (although many of these were forgeries!). Please note – William had the <u>manors</u> recorded, not the <u>parishes</u>. The survey was, of course, Domesday Book 1086.

Domesday Book surveyors worked to a template. William wanted to know how much revenue he could extract from his kingdom and much of the detail is irrelevant to our study of woods. Woods are mentioned, and in some parts of the country they are given dimensions, but in West Berkshire they are described by the number of pigs they could support. This is not very helpful, but clearly a small number of pigs infers a small area of woodland. For example Compton at the head of the Pang Valley had *woodland at 6 pigs* and Kintbury's two manors had *woodland at 3 pigs* and *woodland at 10 pigs* Only one of the four manors at Bucklebury had *woodland at 100 pigs* while the other three had none[30].

There was very little woodland – even in areas that are now well wooded. Place name evidence[31] confirms this. To take the Pang Valley as an example, the Domesday village names are *Compton* – valley farm; *Aldworth* – old enclosures; *Hampstead Norreys* – Home Farm; *Frilsham* – Frithel's farm; *Yattendon* – Geat's people's hollow: *Bucklebury* – Burghild's fort; *Stanford Dingley* – Stoney ford; *Bradfield* – Broad field. Only along the western rim are

<hr>

[30] Morris J (ed) (1979) Domesday Book – Berkshire

[31] Ekwall E. (1974) The Concise Oxford Dictionary of English Place-names.

there names indicating woodland. Chieve*ley*, Lang*ley*, Ils*ley*. And this forest may have given Berkshire its name – *The Forest of Berroc*[32].

What does all this amount to?

Firstly it means that when we look at a wood and admire its trees and flowers we must remember that **at some time everywhere has been cleared**.

Secondly it means that **all woods exist due to the commission or omission of their owners or of the community around them**.

And it is to this we must now turn.

---

[32] Gelling M & Cole A (1974) The Place names of Berkshire Part III 837

Figure 36. A hazel coppice with all the signs of ancientness.

Chapter 4

The development of woods.

Before the modern era, mankind was heavily dependent on woodland. It sheltered the prey of hunter-gatherers and provided the weapons for the hunt. Every farmer, from the Neolithic farmer with a wooden-handled stone-bladed hoe to the mid 20th century farmer, relied on woodland products. Only the development of plastics changed this. For everyone trees and shrubs provided firewood for warmth and for cooking, timber for tools and building material to make shelters for protection from the elements. No matter how great the hunger for farming land, not all the woodland could be cleared.

Timber and wood were harvested from woodland in three main ways, all of which provided them on a continuous cycle that did not destroy the wood.

First in importance was **coppicing**. Coppicing involves cutting through the stem of a young deciduous tree near ground level and then harvesting the poles that sprout from the stump when they reach the required size. To encourage the poles to grow straight and tall the stumps – called stools – are positioned close together. Once a coppice (or 'copse') was established it was valuable and was rarely grubbed out. A side effect of this regime was that the lack of soil disturbance and the alternating periods of light and shade preserved much of the flora of the pre-copse landscape.

Coppicing was certainly being practised by the early Neolithic farmers in the early 4th millennium BC when they made the woven trackways to link islands in the bogs of the Somerset Levels. One length of these has been dated by dendrochronology to about 3,900BC[33]. The vast number of even aged hazel, ash and oak timbers in its construction could not have been gathered by casual selection in ordinary woods. They must have come from managed coppices.

Figure 37. A newly cropped pollard.

ackham O. (2006) *Woodlands*. 280

Figure 38. A very ancient ash stool on a coppice boundary bank amid dense bluebells. The red bar is one metre long and the stool may be almost 1,000 years old.

Land hunger could be partially satisfied by pollarding the young trees rather than coppicing them. **_Pollarding_** involves cutting the young tree above the reach of grazing animals, at (say) 2m or 3m above the ground. The stump is then called a bolling. Once again the resulting poles were harvested when they reached the size needed for the task in hand, whether construction or firewood. The advantage of pollards is that animals can be grazed around them. The tree shade will reduce the value of the grazing, but then one cannot have everything!

Both coppicing and pollarding, if regularly carried out, make the tree almost immortal. The stool or the bolling continues to grow in size as each new crop is taken and can provide evidence of its age – as will be explained later.

Usually, for convenience, copses and pollard trees were maintained within reach of settlements; the superb pollards in Savernake Forest are excellent examples. In the post medieval period individually named pollards were allocated to particular houses to supply timber and firewood[34]. Pollards are usually in hedges and on open commons. Pollards within a modern wood probably indicate that it was a common when they were created.

---

[34] Macnair A &Williamson. T (2010) *William Faden and Norfolk's 18th Century Landscape.*126–128

The third of the most usual ways to manage a wood was **coppice with standards** in which standard trees, ie un-lopped trees, were planted at wide spacings among the coppice stools. The coppice, being lower than a standard tree, shaded its lower trunk and forced it to grow tall and straight to reach the light. It also suppressed the growth of side branches and thus produced straight knot free timber.

Further away from settlements, more natural woodland continued to flourish, particularly on the acid soils of the chalk dip slopes where extremely low pH values (<4.0) made arable farming impossible. It was still of great value to local communities as a source of timber, grazing for horses and cattle in the summer and forage for pigs in the autumn. We have already seen that Bucklebury ran a hundred pigs in 1086. In the early medieval period when populations were low, these areas were pasture woodland, kept open by the grazing, but as populations grew many of them were over-grazed and became virtually treeless areas where only gorse and heather could survive. Hungerford, Snelsmore and Bucklebury give a spread of examples. Ashampstead Common – now wooded – was described as a wood with rights of pasture in the 13th century but by 1761 had become Ashampstead Heath[35].

A major event in Woodland History occurred in 1235 at Merton near London where King Henry III's court had met because Westminster was flooded. A group of senior nobles managed to persuade the king to issue a statute allowing them to enclose Manorial Waste. The nobles themselves must have been persuaded by their Estate Managers that the rapidly growing population was

[35] Greenaway D. (2013) From Pasture Woodland … to Cultural Severance In: Rotherham I.D. (Ed) Cultural Severance and the Environment (2013) 235.

Figure 39. The 1000 year old Cathedral Oak pollard standing on a Savernake boundary bank. (Savernake is actually in Wiltshire – but only just over the border!).

eating into the woodland resource and that the 'open for general use' pasture woodland had to be saved from extinction and be better managed. Kings quite often played the nobility off against the gentry – almost all of whom would have held land from the nobles – and Henry would have been reluctant to upset the *status quo*. Very powerful evidence must have been brought to persuade him.

Anyone who has had to persuade a senior manager in a large organisation to enact a course of action which is of no benefit to the senior manager personally and will probably cause trouble for the said senior manager, will understand how difficult this can be and how important the action must be if the persuasion is to succeed. The resulting Statute of Merton[36] is, in my opinion, the most important document we have for the early history of English woodland. Had it not been issued and implemented our countryside would look very different and be very much less interesting. Because I think it is so important I have included a transcript I made of an 18th century translation held by the Bodleian Library in Oxford. This was made for use by lawyers and was as near as I was able to get to the original document which I was unable to trace. I have retained the 18th century spelling.

[Statute of Merton 23 January 1235]

Provisiones de Merton Anno vicesimo Henrici III

It was provided in the court of our Lord the King, holden at Merton Wednesday the morrow after the feast of St Vincent the 20th year of the Reign of King Henry the son of King John, before the archbishop of Canterbury, and other his bishops and suffragans, and before the greater part of the Earls and barons of England, there being assembled for the Coronation of the said king, and Hellianor (sic) the Queen, about which they were all called, where it was treated for the Commonwealth of the Realm upon the Articles under-written, thus it was provided and granted, as well of the foresaid Archbishops, Bishops, Earls and barons, as of the King himself and others.

CAP IV In what cases Lords may approve against their tenants.

Also because many great men of England (which have enfeoffed Knights, and their freeholders of small Tenements in their great Manors) have complained that they cannot make their profit of the residue of their Manors, as of Wastes, Woods and pastures, whereas the same Feoffees have sufficient Pasture, as much as belongeth to their Tenements; it is provided and granted, That whenever such Feoffees do bring an Assise of Novel disseisin for their Common of Pasture, and it is knowledged before the Justicers, that they have as much pasture as suffices to their Tenements, and that they have free Egress and Regress from their Tenement unto the Pasture, then let them be contented there with; and they on whom it was complained shall go quit of as much as they have made their Profit of their Lands, Wastes, Woods and Pastures; and if they allege that they have not sufficient Pasture, or sufficient Ingress and Egress according to their Hold, then let the Truth be inquired by Assise; and if it be found by Assise, that the same Deforceors have disturbed them of their Ingress or Egress, or that they have not sufficient Pasture (as before is said) then they shall recover their Seisin by view of the Inquest; so that by their Discretion and Oath

---

[36] Ruffhead O. (1786) *The Statutes at Large from Magna Carta to the 25th year of the Reign of King George III* Bodleian Library, Oxford (un-published)

the Plaintiffs shall have sufficient Pasture, and sufficient Ingress and Egress in form aforesaid; and the Disseisor shall be amerced, and shall yield damages, as they were wont before this Provision. And it be certified by the Assise, that the plaintiff has sufficient Pasture, with Ingress and Egress, as before said, let the other make their Profit of the residue, and go quit of that Assise.

The meaning of this tangled language is that Lords of Manors could enclose areas of pasture woodland, in which manorial tenants formerly had free rein, in order to manage them more effectively; with the proviso that the tenants retained sufficient pasture to support their activities and the enclosure did not stop them getting to their tenancies.

The Statute of Merton led to a marked increase in the number of deer parks constructed and to the enclosure and better management of coppices. Judging by the size of some of the coppice stools on their banks a large percentage of West Berkshire's most beautiful bluebell coppices seem to have been created at about this time.

There were several more Acts of Parliament in 1483, 1544 and 1558[37] but these were mainly aimed at protecting the new shoots (the spring) after the coppice had been harvested. The Acts defined how, and for how long, the coppice should be fenced to exclude grazing animals.

Figure 40. Probable 13th century ash coppice stool in dense bluebells on a coppice boundary bank.

---

[37] Tubbs C.R. (1964) *Early Encoppicements of the New Forest*, Forestry 37 (1) 95–105

The 1483 Act extended the period to seven years and the Statute for the Preservation of Woods in 1544 addressed a supposed national timber shortage and the Introduction explains the necessity for the Act:

> *The King perceiving great decay of timber and woods, so that unless speedy remedy be provided, there is great likeli¬hood of scarcity of timber for houses, ships for the whole community.*

The 1544 Act required that coppices retain twelve uncut standard trees per acre, not felled until 10 inches diameter. Young coppices had to be enclosed to exclude grazing animals for four years; those over 14 years for six, and older coppices for seven years. The Act of 1558 extended the closure to nine years. The problem of enforcing these Acts without an organized police force reduced their effectiveness, but the perceived need for the Acts demonstrates the apparently parlous states the woodland had got into. We should also remember Oliver Rackham's opinion that medieval legislation was enacted to provide revenue for the king – not to govern the country! However, the Statute of Merton does not define license fees or fines.

Clearly not all coppice stools and pollards are as huge and dramatic as those illustrated in Figures 38 – 41 so the following will give a better idea of what to expect in most woods and hedges.

Figure 41. Beech coppice stool.

Figure 42. Hazel coppice stools, leaves and nuts.

This newly established, and rather short, ash pollard is in its third year of growth. The bolling is only about 1.5m tall but the spring has survived the attentions of passing horses and a large population of muntjak and roe deer.

Figure 43. New ash coppice. Last cut 3 years ago and a newly established ash pollard.

Figure 44. Ancient but thriving ash coppice stools with details of bark and leaves.

Figure 45. Alder coppice stool with details of bark and leaf.

Figure 46. Field maple coppice stool with details of bark and leaf.

Figure 47. This oak pollard is about 250 years old. Note the scars and knobbles at the junction of the branches with the trunk. These are the result of repeated lopping.

Figure 48. Beech pollards in Moccas Park, Herefordshire. These trees are recorded in the estate records and were established in 1790. Their girth in the late 1990s was 4.9m. The red bar is 1metre long.

Figure 49. Wyatt's Wheelwright's Yard in Yattendon. c.1900. The picture shows newly felled logs, wooden wheels awaiting repair and a selection of carts and timbers of every kind – all of which would have been cut from local woods and copses.

Figure 50. Felling trees in a Pang Valley wood. Yattendon Estates.

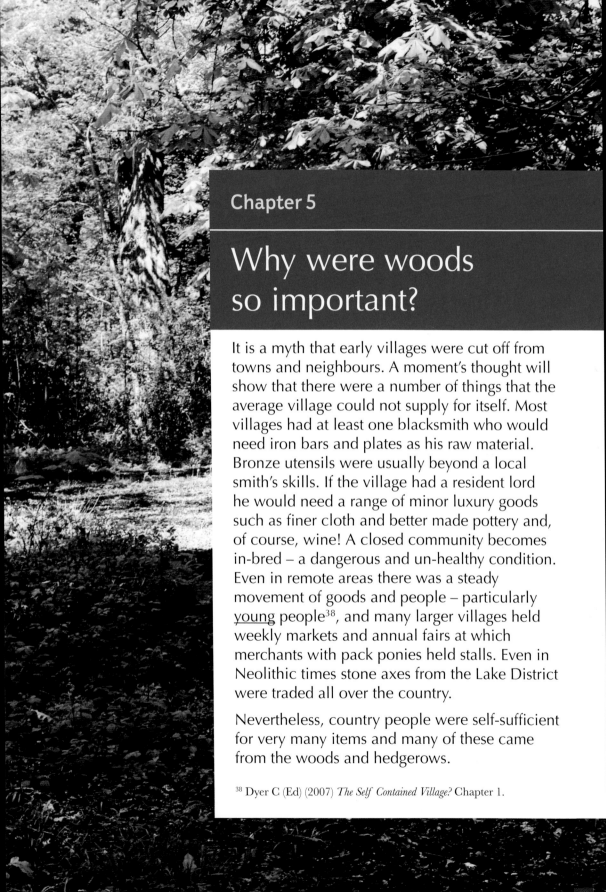

Chapter 5

Why were woods so important?

It is a myth that early villages were cut off from towns and neighbours. A moment's thought will show that there were a number of things that the average village could not supply for itself. Most villages had at least one blacksmith who would need iron bars and plates as his raw material. Bronze utensils were usually beyond a local smith's skills. If the village had a resident lord he would need a range of minor luxury goods such as finer cloth and better made pottery and, of course, wine! A closed community becomes in-bred – a dangerous and un-healthy condition. Even in remote areas there was a steady movement of goods and people – particularly <u>young</u> people[38], and many larger villages held weekly markets and annual fairs at which merchants with pack ponies held stalls. Even in Neolithic times stone axes from the Lake District were traded all over the country.

Nevertheless, country people were self-sufficient for very many items and many of these came from the woods and hedgerows.

[38] Dyer C (Ed) (2007) *The Self Contained Village?* Chapter 1.

Charcoal

Going back to our resident blacksmiths, until coal became cheap and easy to acquire in the 18th century ALL blacksmiths used charcoal and there were sometimes several smiths in a village. Therefore the demand was high and sustained. Charcoal does not travel well. Load a couple of sacks of fresh charcoal pieces on a pack pony and jolt it more than a few miles along a rutted country lane and you will arrive at your destination with two sacks of charcoal dust. So charcoal burners were thick on the ground. 'Colliers Copse' and 'Coleridge Copse' are two Pang Valley wood names and both refer to charcoal burning, but similar names occur all over West Berkshire. Charcoal burners were *colliers* and the sites of their stacks were called *pitsteads* but they had many other names.

Leather making chemicals

Before the invention of plastics and man-made fibres, leather was used for a vast range of purposes – not only for boots and shoes, gloves and coats but also for harness and saddles, buckets and drinking mugs. The list goes on. The farmers and the local butcher supplied the animal hides but the woods supplied the tannery with chemicals to turn a hide into tough, water resistant leather. The most important of these was **tannin**[39] made by soaking ground up oak bark. Oak trees were peeled in May when the bark was rich in tannin and the tree felled later in the year. Again 'Tanners Copse' is a common name.

Potash is a substance not commonly associated with woods. It was one of the oldest industrial chemicals and was used by the ancient Greeks. It was made by burning the waste wood, undergrowth and bracken collected during woodland operations until they were reduced to a fine papery ash with a minimum of carbon. Like so many crafts carried on by illiterate people the process was undocumented and forgotten. It came to an end when better quality potash was imported in quantity and more cheaply from North America and Scandinavia in the 1830s.

A rare record was made in 1736 by James Dunbar[40]. It comes from Scotland but represents the practice in the rest of Britain.

> *Start the fire lay on a cart load or two [in this case of bracken] .. ensure they do not flame ..;when near burnt down steer [stir] up from the bottom …steer frequently until they turn white … make a sconce [windbreak] of brackens to the windward to prevent the ashes blowing away. If there comes a deal of rain you must house or hut*

---

[39] Sturt G. *The wheelwright's shop* (1993) 25.

[40] Rymer.L. (1976) *The history and ethnobotany of bracken* in *The Botanical Journal of the Linnean Society* 73: 151–176

them [cover the ashes]. *If you burn for more than one day, cover the ashes at night. They will burn themselves for some days, till all turn white, and be sure they will be turned twice or thrice a day from the bottom to the top, and they will be whiter; then when they are cold sift and barrel them.*

Next the ash in the barrel was soaked with water. Later the water was drawn off as the decidedly dangerous substance *lye*. It was made in quantity for tanners who soaked the raw hides in it at the start of the tanning process. After a short period in the lye vat the hair could be easily scraped off the hides.

Once again 'lye' is not an unusual element in wood names. Ashampstead parish in the east of West Berkshire has 'Lye Wood' and Hartridge Lye Wood'.

Soap making

Lye was also used by soap makers who boiled it up with lime and animal fat to make a coarse, cheap soap which did the same to the user's hands as the tanner's vat did to the hides. Washerwomen were noted for their reddened and sore hands. Again my examples are from other parts of the country but they would have been common practise in West Berkshire as well.

A 15th century recipe for white soap:

Fern ash was mixed with un-slaked lime to produce a lye which was to stand for two days. It was then strained into a metal kettle, mixed with oil and tallow and made hot. Finally it was mixed with bean flour and moulded by hand.

In 1271 three men and a woman are recorded as working in woods in Staffordshire burning birch, lime and other trees to make ash for sale to dyers.

Celia Fiennes in 1695 describes that, at Wolseley, fern was burned in July, and the ash made into little balls and kept

to make Lye for driving their buck of cloth's which whitens them much.

In Cannock Chase (Kank Wood) the ashes were rolled into balls and sold to be used throughout the year for washing and scouring.

In the 1830s in the Forest of Dean, women went into the woods day after day to cut and burn the green fern

to make ley to put into hard water to wash our clothes and the clothes of the aristocracy.

Glass making.

Although I have not come across any records of glass making in West Berkshire, it seems sensible to complete the wood ash story with a short account of how this woodland product was made.

The most important early glass making area in southern England was in the woods of the Weald of Kent and analysis has shown that all Weald glass was potash glass. Glass cannot be made with sand alone. A flux is needed to lower the melting point of the sand, to make the molten glass workable and to produce a stable product.

Glass is made of roughly 75% silica (usually sand), 10% lime, 15% sodium or potassium oxide (flux). The basic composition of a batch – sand and vegetable ash (containing lime) – has changed little from the earliest times. Potash glass, such as that from the English forests, was of poorer quality than the soda glass from the southern or Mediterranean lands[41]. Theophilus, a German Benedictine monk, possibly writing in the early 12th century, confirms the use of potash in the north by saying

> If you should decide to make glass, first cut plenty of beechwood logs and dry them. Then burn them together in a clean spot and carefully collect the ashes taking care not to mix any earth or stone[42].

It is reasonably certain that the early Weald glassmakers used the ash from beech and oak billets with which their furnaces were fired, supplemented by the ash of other inland plants including bracken, and there are numerous angry comments from glassmakers about delayed supplies and the poor quality of local woodland ashes[43]. The type of wood used to make the ash governed the colour of the glass. For instance, beech ash gave the glass a pink tinge and elm a dark blue[44].

Wheelwrights and Carpenters.

These highly skilled craftsmen did not get their timber from Latvia via B&Q. They went into the woods with templates in their hands[45] and chose the trees that would suit the task – not the one in hand, but the one that would start in a couple of years time when the timber had been seasoned. House builders chose their timber in the same way but worked it green, choosing the tree or sapling nearest in size to the beam they needed (see Figure 51). Even quite a small house would need a hundred or more trees of various sizes[46].

---

[41] *A History of Technology Vol 3* OUP 1957

[42] *De Diversis Atribus. Theophilus.* Ed CR Dodswell Nelson 1961 Book 2 Sect 3 57

[43] Kenyon. GH. *The Glass Industry of the Weald* 1967 Leicester University Press 38

[44] Jobling. Matt. National Glass Centre. *Personal communication*

[45] Sturt G. *The wheelwright's shop* (1993) 25

[46] Rackham. O. (2006) *Woodlands* 290.

Figure 51. This beam was formed by squaring a single small oak tree about 40cm (15″) in diameter. It was inserted in the late 16th century.

Figure 52. This great curving cruck is one of a pair made by sawing a tree down the middle.

59

Medieval tools would not have coped with iron-hard seasoned oak and this is the main reason that reused ships timbers were NOT brought miles from the ports to make the curved crucks like the one shown in Figure 52. There are records of timber from wrecks being used to make sheds etc along the East Anglian coast but these would have been planks and possibly timber from the cargoes[47].

Furniture.

Oak and elm were the usual timbers for furniture making until about the 18th century when expensive foreign timbers such as mahogany became available. Beech became very popular for cheaper furniture in the mid 1800s when Windsor chairs became fashionable.

The oak and elm were generally drawn from quick grown hedgerow or parkland trees and were worked in town workshops. Because furniture makers required relatively small quantities of timber they tended to buy seasoned timber from timber yards and, in country areas, from wheelwrights. Beech legs and rails were made and stacked to season in the woods before being assembled in town factories. They were also sold in some of the first 'flat packs' for home assembly and were exported as far as New Zealand. Some of them were no more reliable than their modern equivalent. There were angry reports of people landing on the floor when they sat on a chair and the seat collapsed!

Examples of oak furniture still in daily use.

Figure 53. A 16th century oak coffer.

Figure 54. A 17th century court cupboard.

---

[47] Defoe D. (1724–6). *A Tour through the Whole Island of Great Britain*. Penguin Classics 1986. 94

Sawyers.

The sawyers who cut up the felled trees were a race apart and George Sturt gives the best contemporary account of them in his classic book *The Wheelwright's Shop*[48]. They were independent itinerant men who worked in pairs using tools owned by the top sawyer. In the summer they went around the woodland estates sawing felled timber in the woods for gateposts and rails and other tasks on the estate. They used sawpits previously dug for them near the logs to be cut[49]. In the winter they moved to the villages where the wheelwright's yard or the builder's yard would have a brick lined sawpit with a roof. It is difficult to imagine a more tedious job. The log was firmly clamped along the centre of the sawpit and the top sawyer stood on top of the log and guided the long two-handed saw. The bottom sawyer stood in the pit underneath the log in a continuous shower of sawdust and pulled and lifted the bottom of the saw. Imagine doing this from six o'clock in the morning to six o'clock in the evening, day after day! It was no wonder that they were great drinkers and that it was often difficult to get them both sober enough at the same time to start work.

Figure 55. A sawpit in use. Museum of English Rural Life University of Reading.

---

[48] Sturt G. *The wheelwright's shop* (1993) 38

[49] Tyson. B. (no date) *Oak, from Woodland Sawpits to Ships* in The Quarterly Journal of Forestry.

Another craft – although the list is not in any way complete – was clog making[50].

Clog making.

There was a considerable market for clogs in industry and dairying and anywhere where people had to work on wet floors. A clog is a shoe with a solid wooden sole and leather uppers, unlike the continental *sabot* where both sole and uppers are carved from a single piece of wood. Many different woods were used for clog soles but alder was very popular. It is rot resistant, easy to carve when green, and light when seasoned. Alder plantations can be made in wet, poorly drained land, which would otherwise be useless. Like the chair bodgers, the clog makers cut the alder stems and rough-carved and seasoned the blocks on site. When dry, the blocks were moved to workshops where they were carved into the various sizes needed.

Alder was also used for scaffold poles and its charcoal was part of the formula for pistol-grade gunpowder. Alder plantations and coppice stools are not uncommon along the Pang, Kennet and lower Lambourn. A good example is Bull Pate at the north end of Paices Wood Country Park just south of Aldermaston.

Figure 56. Ben Palmer making ash gate hurdles on Ashampstead Common.

---

[50] Edlin HL (1973) *Woodland Crafts in Britain*. 24. (This the classic account)

Figure 57. Rake making. Museum of English Rural Life University of Reading.

Other Woodland crafts.

Beyond all these there were, of course, other woodland crafts producing items needed in everyday life.

The tools used by the farmer were often made in the woods using the local poles and timber[51]. Simple shelters were set up. A pole lathe made from a springy sapling was erected to turn rounded items. A vice – called a *horse* – might be made to hold timber firmly while it was worked on[52]. The Lailey family of Bucklebury Common were famous for their wooden bowls and thousands of hazel hurdles and ash gate hurdles were made to pen sheep and to protect new hedges.

The two classic books are *Woodland Crafts of Britain* by Herbert L Edlin – first published in 1949 – and *Country Craft Tools* by Percy W Blandford – first published in 1974. Herbert Edlin worked among the dying crafts recording them and photographing them. There are many modern books on the subject and their information is usually drawn from Edlin. Percy W Blandford's photographs and line drawings are accurate and comprehensive.

---

[51] Edlin HL (1973) *Woodland Crafts in Britain.*

[52] Blandford PW (1974) *Country Craft Tools* 128 (This is the classic account)

Lime burning

Although not strictly a woodland product, lime was often made in, or on the edge of, chalkland woods where the quarries were dug to avoid using good arable land. The main purpose of the quarries was to provide raw chalk to spread on the surrounding acid soils in order to raise their pH to a level where cereals could be grown. This had been practised since Roman times and should not be confused with *marling*. Marling is the spreading of calcareous clays and shelly deposits on acid sandy soils to both sweeten them and give them bulk. Both chalking and marling died out in the mid 19th century when cheap bulk supplies of lime made in industrial limekilns became readily available. At about the same time, it was found that grassland improved with chalk was injurious to sheep grazed on it and, as a result, farmers switched to *maglime* made from magnesium limestone.

As a secondary product to the production of raw chalk, the quarrymen made small quantities of lime near the quarry by burning chalk in **farmers' limekilns** using the readily available wood fuel. Like potash making, this is another craft that died out before it was recorded.

A small, deep, steep sided pit was dug near the quarry with one or more narrow trenches to let air into the bottom. Block chalk was then laid in layers interspersed with layers of wood fuel. The mass was then set on fire and burned very fiercely. The walls and rim of the pit got extremely hot. Tests with a magnetometer on a number of pits have made this very clear. The heat converted the chalk into **quicklime** – a very dangerous substance that had to be quenched with quantities of water before it could be used. The resulting **slaked lime** was used to make mortar for building work and lime-wash for painting walls etc. where it had the added benefit of killing insect life and acting as a general disinfectant.

Firewood

On wooded commons firewood collecting was a right of the commoners. Otherwise firewood came from trees and shrubs growing in hedges not in woods – although 'lop and top' from forestry operations was sold as bundles of twigs called bavins. Farmers used hedges as long narrow woods and planted and pollarded the trees in them to supply the farm with logs and faggots. One of the early farm manuals, *500 Points of Good Husbandry*[53] written by Thomas Tusser in 1557 tells the farmer:

> *From Maie til October leave cropping, for why? In wood sere, whatsoever thou croppest wil dy*

---

[53] Tusser T. (1557 reprinted 1984) *Five Hundred Points of Good Husbandry* 74,75

This means that if you cut the canopy off a tree in the dry summer it will die.

Under January's Husbandry, *Lopping of pollengers* [pollards].

Now lop for thy fewell old pollenger growen,
that hinder the corne or the grasse to be mowen.
In lopping and felling, save edder and stake,
thine hedges as needeth to mend or to make.

In lopping old Jocham, for feare of mishap,
one bough stay unlopped, to cherish the sap:
The second year after then boldly ye may,
for driping his fellows, that bough cut away.

This means: lop the large boughs off a hedgerow pollard – which may be shading the crop in the field alongside it – when it is leafless and dormant in January. But leave one large bough to start the new canopy. Lop this bough when the canopy has reformed. Old pollards sometimes still have a bough that survived when pollarding was given up.

Health care

Before health care became scientific, both professional apothecaries and amateurs gathered medicinal plants from the fields and woods. The ending *wort* to a plant's name generally indicates a medicinal use – *figwort*, *stitchwort* and *St John's Wort*. The elder bush provided medicine from its flowers and its berries – as well as wines from both. Rosehips from brambles are richer in vitamin C than oranges and were collected during World War 2 and before to make a syrup as a cold cure.

The strange 'Doctrine of Signatures' was used by physicians and apothecaries to decide which remedy to apply to a disease. Basically, if a plant looked like part of the body then it would cure the diseases of that part. For example, since a *walnut* has a hard case like a skull containing a nut that looks like a brain, then a medicine made from it must be good for problems of the head. *Lungwort (pulmonaria officinalis)* has leaf patterns that look like lung tissue and therefore must be good for lung problems. This may sound horribly dangerous to us, but some of the nostrums did actually work. A medicine made from oak bark did actually help in cases of diarrhoea and a decoction of St Johns Wort is still used to sooth depression. *Digitalis* made from foxgloves was used to make a heart stimulant until quite recently when it was synthesised.

However, they are certainly NOT 'something to try at home'!

Figure 58. Elder – the country medicine chest.

Figure 59. St John's wort.

Figure 60. Rosehips.

Figure 61. Foxgloves.

Figure 62. A deer park pale (boundary bank) licensed in 1336.

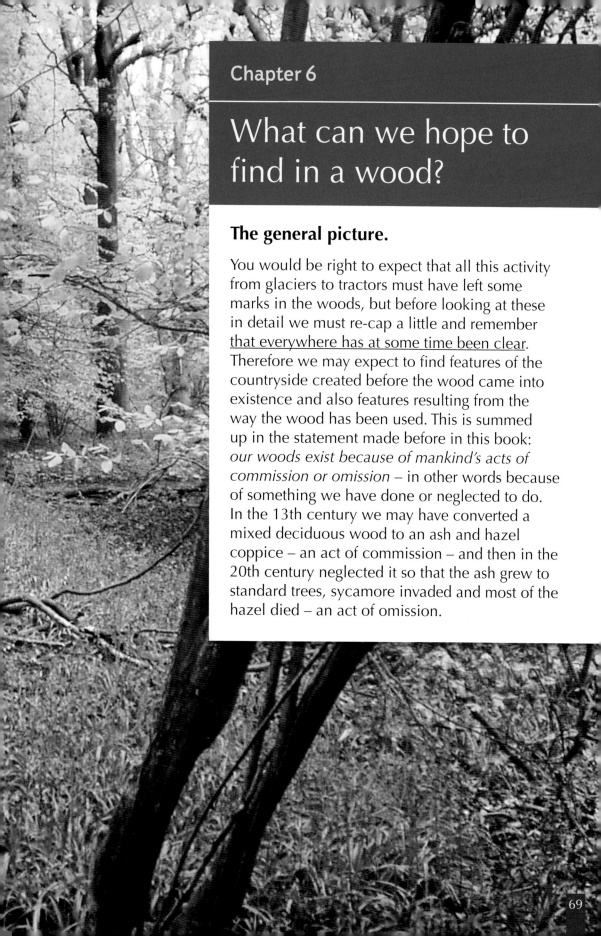

Chapter 6

What can we hope to find in a wood?

The general picture.

You would be right to expect that all this activity from glaciers to tractors must have left some marks in the woods, but before looking at these in detail we must re-cap a little and remember that everywhere has at some time been clear. Therefore we may expect to find features of the countryside created before the wood came into existence and also features resulting from the way the wood has been used. This is summed up in the statement made before in this book: *our woods exist because of mankind's acts of commission or omission* – in other words because of something we have done or neglected to do. In the 13th century we may have converted a mixed deciduous wood to an ash and hazel coppice – an act of commission – and then in the 20th century neglected it so that the ash grew to standard trees, sycamore invaded and most of the hazel died – an act of omission.

Many woods exist because their soils made them unattractive to early farmers. Many of the ridges between our dry valleys and river valleys are covered with very acid clay and flint, gravels and sands – washout from the glaciers. Some have pH values as low as 3.5 and, since a pH of at least 7 is needed to grow cereals, they have been left to grow trees. Some were cleared to make rough grazing land and were later planted up with conifers.

Older woods can be expected to contain more pre-wood features than younger woods because there had been less time for a feature to be destroyed before the wood covered it.

When you consider the range of ancient features in the open areas of the West Berkshire countryside – from Neolithic long barrows, Bronze Age round barrows, Iron Age hillforts to World War 2 remains – it seems obvious that the wooded areas should have similar features. Without doubt many historic features remain to be discovered in our woods because for the last few centuries

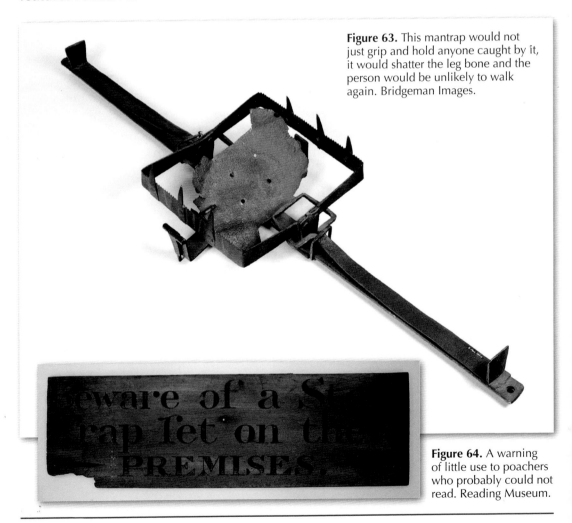

Figure 63. This mantrap would not just grip and hold anyone caught by it, it would shatter the leg bone and the person would be unlikely to walk again. Bridgeman Images.

Figure 64. A warning of little use to poachers who probably could not read. Reading Museum.

many woods have been privately owned and fiercely guarded. Many have still not been systematically explored and the hidden features mapped. If you find this level of protectiveness hard to believe just think of ditched, banked and fenced medieval deer parks and the penalties for being caught in one. Think of 18th and 19th century pheasant coverts guarded by gamekeepers and provided with hidden mantraps to deter poachers who faced transportation if captured.

In addition, of course, the very fact that the features are covered with trees and bushes, brambles and bracken, makes it even more likely that they will not have been noticed and recorded. Aerial photography has made the mapping of ancient features in farmland something that can be done in the comfort of a warm dry study, but until recently aerial survey instruments could not penetrate vegetation and the only option was cold, damp winter survey on the ground. The introduction of LiDAR surveys has improved on this, but it is still necessary to ground truth the findings and this still means getting cold and muddy! Surveying will be discussed in more detail in a later chapter.

Definition of an Ancient Wood.

An Ancient Wood is defined as a wood that can be shown to have existed in 1600. It is considered that, because there was little organised creation of plantations before this date, a wood already in existence in 1600 had probably existed in some form for a long time before 1600. This does not mean that it has links going back to the prehistoric Wildwood. Few, if any, woods in the southern part of England can be shown to have links going back that far. However, because of the simplicity of machinery and woodland management techniques in the early periods, less damage was done to the features and flora – particularly the ground flora – during woodland work and so more of it may have survived than in the landscape around the wood.

It may seem a strange thing to say, **but trees are almost irrelevant when defining ancient woods – it is the <u>ground flora</u> that identifies an Ancient Wood**. As said before, trees are subject to market forces. While there is a demand for hazel hurdles, hazel coppices will flourish, only to be converted to oak woodland when the market demands oak. But all the time the ground flora grows on, subject to pressures of shading and grazing, but still flowering and seeding as it has done every year for millennia while the wood changes around it.

This is particularly true of those plants with poor seed dispersal abilities. If they are destroyed they are unlikely to return and these are the **Ancient Woodland Indicator Species**. The more of these species you find in a wood the more likely it is to have a long history as woodland.

The Thames Valley Environmental Records Centre[54] has made a special study of West Berkshire woods and has developed a more focussed list, but for the non-botanist, for the more general woodland explorer, it is possible to say that if there are a lot of different flowers growing in your wood it is quite likely to be ancient – particularly if they are the kinds that do not spread rapidly. Bluebells are a slightly shaky indicator but <u>very dense</u> bluebells are likely to have been there for a long time. Oliver Rackham observed that, in East Anglia, bluebells spread at about a metre a century and my surveys in West Berkshire point in the same direction. Wood anemones (known to my children when small as *wooden enemies*) are good indicators. Their seed is rarely fertile. They spread via rhizomes and once destroyed rarely return. Distant from habitations, primroses suggest ancientness as does the delicate, easily recognised grass, wood melick.

Ancient Woodland Indicator Species.

These vary with the part of the country you are in. You would hardly expect to find the same suite of flowers growing in a warm damp southern county as halfway up a mountain in Wales. In this book we are primarily concerned with West Berkshire and the table in Figure 65 has been made from a general list published by Natural England for Southern Britain.

Species most strongly associated with Ancient Woodland and which are typical of botanically rich ancient woodland communities.

Moschatel	Green hellebore	Common cow-wheat
Ransoms	Wood barley	Wood melick
Wood anemone	Bluebell	Wood millet
Hard fern	Tutsan	Three-veined sandwort
Smooth-stalked sedge	Stinking iris	Wild daffodil
Thin-spiked wood sedge	Yellow archangel	Birdsnest orchid
	Toothwort	Early purple orchid
Lily of the valley	Southern wood-rush	Goldenrod
Spurge laurel	Hairy woodrush	Guelder rose
Narrow buckler fern	Great woodrush	Bush vetch
Scaly male fern	Yellow pimpenell	Wood vetch
Violet helleborine	Primrose	Marsh violet
Wood spurge	Crab apple	Early dog violet
Woodruff		

[54] Thames Valley Environmental Records Centre, Signal Court, Eynsham, OX29 4TL
www.tverc.org

Wood-sorrel	Wild cherry	Marsh Fern
Herb paris	Narrow-leaved lungwort	Small-leaved lime
Hartstongue		Wych Elm
Greater butterfly orchid	Goldilocks buttercup	Bilberry
Wood meadow-grass	Black currant	Wood speedwell
Solomon's seal	Red currant	Pignut
Common polypody	Field rose	Broad-leaved helleborine
Hard shield fern	Butcher's-broom	
Soft shield fern	Sanicle	Narrow-lipped helleborine
Black currant	Wood club-rush	
Red currant	Orpine	
Barren strawberry	Saw-wort	Red – strongly associated.
Aspen	Wild service tree	Green – only if remote from habitations.
Barren strawberry	Betony	
Primrose	Black bryony	Black – closely associated

Figure 65. Ancient Woodland Indicator Species.

A selection of Ancient Woodland Indicator Species.

Figure 66. Wood sorrel.

Figure 67. Green hellebore.

Figure 68. Moschatel (town hall clock).

Figure 69. Our native bluebell.

Figure 70. Tutsan.

Figure 71. Wood anemone.

Figure 72. Ramsons (wild garlic).

Figure 73. Sweet woodruff.

Figure 74. Wood spurge (cup & saucer plant).

Figure 75. Solomon's seal. Cultivated variety.

We have already looked at the purpose of a number of these features in Chapter 5 and we will now discuss what their remains look like in a wood. Repetition is inevitable so please bear with me!

Features from before the wood.

The earliest pre-wood monument I have recorded is a **Bronze Age Round Barrow** in Park Wood at Hampstead Norreys. Round Barrows are burial mounds and date from between about 2500BC and 1200BC. They are very common and are scattered all over the chalk lands. In open country they have usually been ploughed flat. A few have survived, usually damaged, and are now protected as Scheduled Ancient Monuments. The Hampstead Norreys example is one of a cluster of five around the village, four of which are now barely visible. Park Wood has protected the fifth. In 1515 the then Lord of the Manor was summoned by a Commission set up by Cardinal Wolsey to investigate unauthorised enclosures. He had enclosed 30 acres to make a deer park. The enclosure was permitted and became **Park Wood** and was no longer ploughed. As a result the barrow survived in pristine condition. It is a Scheduled Ancient Monument and it is an offence to damage it in any way.

Figure 76. The Bronze Age Barrow in Park Wood. This is a Scheduled Ancient Monument.

Figure 77. The rampart of Grimsbury Castle near Hermitage.

The Iron Age is noted for its **Hillforts**. These, like barrows, are liberally scattered across West Berkshire – generally on hilltops with commanding views. **Grimsbury Castle** near Hermitage is in a wood on a hilltop and would have had excellent views before the woodland phase. It is of the standard construction – a massive earth bank in an approximate circle with a deep, wide ditch on the outside. It was constructed in about 50BC and was probably not permanently occupied. It too is a Scheduled Ancient Monument and is on private land but can be seen from the road. *Grim* was a Saxon by-name for their god Odin. These massive banks were considered too big to have been created by human hands and so the Saxons credited them to the gods.

Iron Age people, and the Bronze Age people before them, made a lot of use of **earth embankments**. Near Aldworth there are a series of **large linear banks and ditches** known as **Grim's Ditch**. They run from the River Thames to a point south of Aldworth village and then stop abruptly. They face north. That is, the ditch is on the north side of the bank. Again, they are Scheduled Ancient Monuments and are on private land but can be seen from the road. Excavators in the 1970s

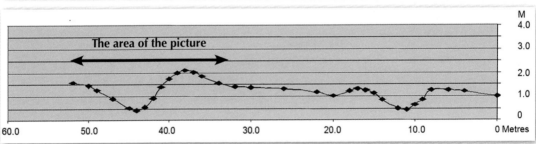

Figure 78. Grim's Ditch near Aldworth. The northern bank and ditch with a measured profile through both boundaries.

found Roman pottery in the sediment that had collected in one ditch and so they were considered to be pre-Roman and probably estate or tribal boundaries. Once again, the best preserved sections are in woods (see Chapter 3). In fields they have been ploughed flat. Detailed winter survey showed that the boundary was actually a double bank and ditch – two banks and ditches running parallel with a flat area between them. The amount of sheer hard manual work needed to create these monuments is hard to imagine.

Figure 79. Grim's Dyke in 1877.

Bowler's Copse

Broom Wood

The western section is along this edge

Figure 80. Grim's Dyke. The central section.

Grim's Dyke, 2½km south east of Grim's Ditch, is one of West Berkshire's mysteries. It is composed of three linked sections of banks and ditches with the ditch on the north see Figure 79. The centre section is very large – as can be seen in Figure 80. The western section is smaller and the eastern section looks as if it was never finished. There is a further possible section beyond the eastern end. The plan of the site does not make sense and, although it looks Iron Age and the *Grim* place name suggests antiquity, no proven date or purpose has ever been put forward. Once again, being in an Ancient Wood has protected Grim's Dyke.

Roman sites tend to be very elusive and I cannot offer a firm example. Some woodland features such as terraces, ponds, boundary banks, and chalk pits may originate in the Roman period, but without the evidence of pottery and tiles and other characteristic debris, it is impossible to claim features as Roman.

Figure 81. Streatley Warren field system banks in 1934.
©Ashmolean Museum University of Oxford.

ATLEY WARREN

Field systems – known as **Celtic Fields** – are common all over the West Berkshire chalk but sadly most of them have been ploughed out in recent years and now only show as soil marks. However, they do occur in some woods. As can be seen from the 1934 aerial photograph of the Streatley Warren field system (Figure 81), the field boundaries outside the wood extend into the wood showing that the wood is more recent than the fields. They were investigated in 1948 and in 1978 and it was found that they were probably created in the Bronze Age and were in use in the Iron Age and the Roman period[55]. The boundary banks were severely damaged by ploughing in World War 2 but survive in pristine condition in the wood and can be seen from a Public Right of Way.

[55] http://archaeologydataservice.ac.uk/archives/view/berks_bas_2007/journal.cfm?volume=51
http://www.heritagegateway.org.uk/Gateway/Results_Single.aspx?uid=MWB3190&resourceID=1030
http://www.heritagegateway.org.uk/Gateway/Results_Single.aspx?uid=MWB7220&resourceID=1030

Figure 82. One of the Streatley Warren field banks in the neighbouring wood.

Figure 83. Terraces in Portugal.

Figure 84. A terrace in woodland.

Connected with early farming are **cultivation terraces**, sometimes known as **strip lynchets**. These are long, narrow, flat 'steps' cut into a hillside and running along the contours. The traditional explanation of these undateable features is that they were caused by land hungry farmers moving onto marginal land when the population exceeded the food supply in the years leading up to the Black Death in 1348. But is this really their origin?

Modern farmers in the area dismiss the idea as very unlikely. They point out that the first ploughing would have loosened the thin layer of topsoil and exposed the raw chalk underneath in which nothing would grow. There would have been no incentive to carry on with the ploughing long enough to form a terrace. So if they are <u>not</u> medieval or earlier plough terraces, what are they and who made them and for what purpose? There are too many of them to have been made by accident and a huge amount of very hard physical work would have been involved. Well, where in the modern world do similar terraces occur?

In my experience they occur all over Italy, Spain and Portugal where they are carefully constructed to grow vines, olive and almond trees and similar crops. Is it possible that the terraces in our woods were made by the same experts for similar purposes – if not for wine, then possibly for orchards, hazel groves etc? Were they constructed during the 400 years of Roman rule or even earlier? In Italy they have been dated as early as the Neolithic Period and shown to have been in use ever since. There they sometimes had to be cut into rock with crowbars and then filled with soil brought up from the valleys on the backs of mules and men[56]. The Iron Age people of southern England had contacts with the Mediterranean lands and their chieftains are known to have had a definite fondness for wine. People capable of creating Maiden Castle in Dorset would have no problems with a vine terrace! If either of these is the case, the 'step' will have been trenched out and filled with topsoil. It would be interesting to monitor the next pipe trench passing through some of them.

[56] Agnoletti M *Valorising the European Rural Landscape* in *Cultural Severance and the Environment* (2013) Rotherham I (Ed) 73

Many, if not most, features we find in woods are undateable. We can hazard a guess but it is rarely possible to be certain. An earthen bank is a bank is a bank and looks much the same if it was built 100 years ago or 2000 years ago. Other examples of this are the ***old, disused roads*** we sometimes find in a wood. It is often possible to say when they went out of use but never, in my experience, to say when they began to be used. Were they cut through an existing wood? In which case they fall into the 'use made of the wood' category. Or were they there before the wood that grew up around them? Many of our country lanes follow natural routes, perhaps kept open by animals and herds moving along them. Think of some of the very narrow lanes winding along our West Berkshire dry valleys. No road engineer ever set them out. At the end of the Ice Age, when the chalk was frozen, streams flowed down the valleys carrying gravels and stones eroded from the uncovered soils. When the streams sank into the chalk they left a thick strip of sands and gravel that, even when covered with hill wash, still made a winding well-drained path along the least gradient. When the trees arrived the users kept the passage open and in the 20th century the gravel was covered with tarmac. So what date are they?

Straight roads were certainly made and not only by the Romans, but until the construction of the Turnpike Roads in the 17th and 18th century their making was rarely recorded.

Figure 85. A medieval road abandoned when a deer park pale was built across it in 1336. The huge ash coppice stools on the road bank show that it was in existence before the park was licensed.

Figure 86. A holloway. Hook End Lane. Basildon.

Holloways are a variation on roads and frequently occur on steep slopes. These deep cut and frequently winding trenches were formed by centuries of wear as feet, hooves and wheels followed the same route up a hill. The loosened soil was washed down by the next rainstorm and the holloway got deeper. If they were tarmaced in the 20th century they became roads, frequently deeper than a car's roof.

Scour lines (large and small) are a variation on holloways! Medieval roads were simple tracks. Few were surfaced in any way. Well-used roads became unuseably muddy in wet weather and road users simply moved to one side. When that route became a swamp they moved to the other side. Over time a fan of wide trenches developed. Eventually one was surfaced and tarmaced and the others became interesting features. They occur in woods on slopes having an ancient road passing through them.

Smaller **scour lines** were caused by logs being dragged out of a wood down a slope – either by a horse or, later, by a tractor. Once a hollow had been created by the first log the others would tend to roll into it and it would get deeper until it became a hindrance and the horseman or tractor driver took another route.

Figure 87. A stock watering pond in an 18th century field.

In Chapter 3 I made the point that right up to the early 19th century the West Berkshire landscape was much more open and un-wooded than it is now. The first really detailed map of the whole of (old) Berkshire was made in 1761[57]. The scale of 2 inches to 1mile allows the detailed depiction of wood and field boundaries and it is clear that many areas now covered with trees were fields and grazing paddocks in the 18th century. As with deer parks, the lack of surface water in much of the West Berkshire landscape meant that **ponds** had to be created for stock watering and these can still exist in the subsequent woods. Like the one in Figure 87, they are usually obviously artificial. This one is perfectly round and has an embanked lower edge.

Continuing the farming theme, some woods have grown up over abandoned early arable land. Medieval farmers often (not always) ploughed their land using the **ridge and furrow system** which left the field looking like a suddenly frozen sea with long low narrow curving ridges separated by shallow hollows.

---

[57] Rocque. John (1761) *A Survey of the County of Berkshire* Headley Bros. Ashford

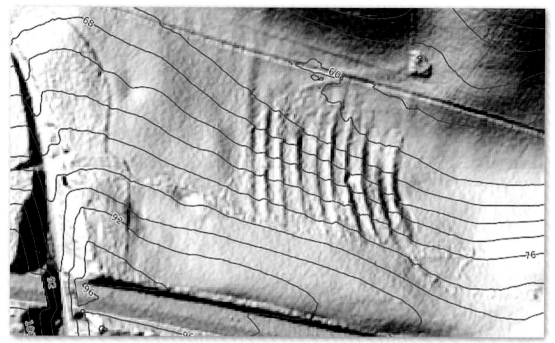

Figure 88. A LiDAR image of ridge and furrow in a wood. Environment Agency Open Data.

This system was used to improve the drainage of heavy land and that was the land most likely to be abandoned and planted with trees. The size of the ridges depended on the length of time they were farmed in that manner. Sometimes they are huge and very obvious but others are quite hard to spot without the help of a low sun. At either end of the ridges and furrows are **headlands**. These are wider and more irregular raised areas where the plough team was turned and the plough scraped clean.

Figure 89. Ridge and furrow highlighted by snow.

The other ridge like feature commonly found in woods is the **_linear bank_**. These are smaller than the massive ranch boundaries described on page 78. Linear banks provide a neat link for features from the 'before the wood' section to the 'during the life of the wood' section because they can belong to either period. They can be remains of early field systems or they can be boundaries created when part of the wood was sold to a new owner. It is often impossible to tell. Even an archaeological excavation would be unlikely to provide evidence for their date of creation. Sometimes a document will turn up recording the sale but these are rare for early periods. A Saxon Charter may refer to them but this will only mean that they were already in existence in the Saxon Period. I know of one bank that runs right through an Ancient Wood and passes near a large Roman site in the open land beyond the wood. The field around the site has almost as much building debris as soil, yet when a windblown tree tore a section through the bank it did not contain a single piece of Roman material. It was clearly there before the Roman period. This is not an isolated occurrence. A boundary bank and ditch forming the northern edge of Whippendell Wood in Hertfordshire is part of a system of boundaries containing unworn Iron Age pottery and is thus prehistoric[58]. It is obviously sensible to use existing features as boundaries rather than go to the expense and effort of building new ones. The Tithe Award map shows that the bank and ditch in Figure 90 marks the boundaries between the manors of Hampstead Norreys, Eling and Wyld[59]. All three manors are recorded in Domesday Book, and so it is reasonable to assume that the bank and ditch existed in 1086. However, they may have existed before that date and marked the boundaries of Saxon, or even earlier, estates.

[58] Williamson T (2010) *The Origins of Hertfordshire.* Hertford University Press. 188.

[59] Peacock D. (2016) Pers Comm. *Hampstead Norreys Tithe Award Map*

Figure 90. A linear bank and ditch in Hampstead Norreys woods marking the boundaries between the Manors of Hampstead Norreys, Eling and Wyld.

Features due to the use made of the wood.

It is not until we get into the post Norman Conquest period that I have been able to put tentative dates to woodland features. As I explained in Chapter 4, early medieval woods tended to be wood pasture and the first readily identifiable and dateable constructions were **deer parks**. There were a few deer parks before 1066 but the greatest growth came after 1235 when the Statute of Merton allowed Lords of Manors to enclose Manorial Waste – which, in West Berkshire and off the high chalk, was likely to be manorial wood pasture. Look for *Park Wood* names. There were thousands of deer parks in England. In 1986 Oliver Rackham estimated there were about 3200 by 1300[60], but many more have been

Deer Park Features

Figure 91. A typical medieval style pale fence.

Figure 92. A park pale and ditch. The park is on the left.

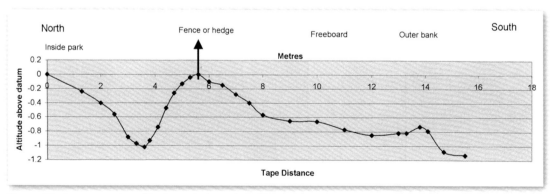

Figure 93. A measured profile through the pale in Figure 92.

---

[60] Rackham. O.(1986) *The History of the Countryside* 123

found since then. If a park was in or near a Royal Forest it had to be licensed by the king and a record may exist, but if not it could be constructed without permission and documentary evidence would be unlikely to survive. However, deer parks had standard components and these are easily recognised. They had to be surrounded by a **pale** to stop the deer escaping. This was usually a substantial bank with a ditch on the <u>inside</u>. The bank would have been topped with a fence (Figures 91 & 92). To allow access to the pale for repairs a track, called the **freeboard**, had to be constructed <u>outside</u> the pale. Many 'Park Lane' road names can be traced to this feature. Parks on West Berkshire's pervious soils needed **ponds** to water the deer and any other livestock that shared the park. Often these had to be lined with clay to contain the water and a falling tree could easily puncture the lining. The drained pond would then become a muddy hollow rapidly filled with leaves but still noticeable – particularly in winter when the ground vegetation is at its lowest. And finally parks need park keepers and **parkers** needed **lodges**. These were usually built where they had a good view over the park, sometimes with a view of an entrance gate or a pond. They were provided with paddocks for the parker's animals – he would need a pony to draw his cart when he checked and repaired the pale. Intensive grazing and trampling would damage the woodland flora and sometimes this can still be seen in the distribution of Ancient Woodland Indicator Species. (See Chapter 7).

Other common features in early deer parks are **pillow mounds** and they are sometimes sited within view of the lodge. They are long low mounds with a ditch on either side. They come in many shapes and sizes, sometimes singly and sometimes in groups[61]. Any isolated short length of bank might be a pillow mound. Pillow mounds were artificial rabbit warrens built to house rabbits when they were introduced from Sicily in the 12th century. These rabbits did not burrow and did not like the British climate and so they were provided with dry frost-proof homes. A network of earth-covered wooden or stone tunnels was made for them to live in. They were very expensive animals and were valued both for their flesh and the fur that was used to trim and line winter clothing.

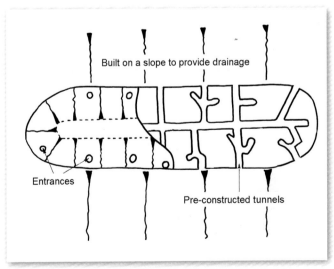

Built on a slope to provide drainage

Entrances

Pre-constructed tunnels

Figure 94. Diagram of a pillow mound.

---

[61] Williamson T (2006) *The Archaeology of Rabbit Warrens.*

Figure 95. A chalk quarry. The white staff is 5m long. The haul ramp is on the left.

In the 13th century a single rabbit would have cost the equivalent of the day's pay of an ordinary workman. They were culled, or harvested, by putting a ferret into the tunnel on one side of the mound to bolt them out of the other side where they were caught in a net.

Features common to all older woods are **holes in the ground** – some big, some small. However, some holes are natural and some are man-made and some are a combination of the two. Nothing is ever simple in Woodland Archaeology! The natural holes are **swallow holes** where streams pour straight into the underground aquifers[62] or **solution holes** formed when underground water dissolves the chalk causing the surface layers to collapse into the cavity. The man-made ones are **chalk quarries, sand pits and gravel pits** and **road material quarries**. To confuse matters, sometimes a quarry provides a route into the chalk and becomes a swallow hole and sometimes a swallow hole is enlarged and becomes a quarry. A rule of thumb for deciding which is which is that man-made holes have a ramp to allow the material to be extracted whereas untouched swallow holes approximate to a smooth conical shape. In floodplain woods you may come upon **peat diggings**. These are shallow irregular holes filled with water, reeds and willows. The wood name can give a lead, for example *Peat Pits Wood* near Sulham in the Pang Valley.

[62] Dunlop L & Greenaway D. (2011) *Around the 3 Valleys.* 172

Figure 96. A road material quarry dug on Ashampstead Common.

Starting with the **bigger man-made holes**. Landowners seemed to be reluctant to use arable land to quarry chalk for their fields, sand for their buildings or gravel for their roads and preferred to dig in their woods although many fields do contain back-filled chalk pits. Parish Councils were responsible for the up-keep of their roads until 1889 and they too preferred to obtain their road making material from their Commons.

Chalk quarries tend to be large and deep and are often cut into a slope to avoid lifting the heavy chalk.

Sand pits, **gravel pits** and **road material quarries** only use the relatively thin surface strata of the Lambeth Group. They went out of general use when the new County Councils took over road maintenance in 1889 and preferred to use commercial quarries.

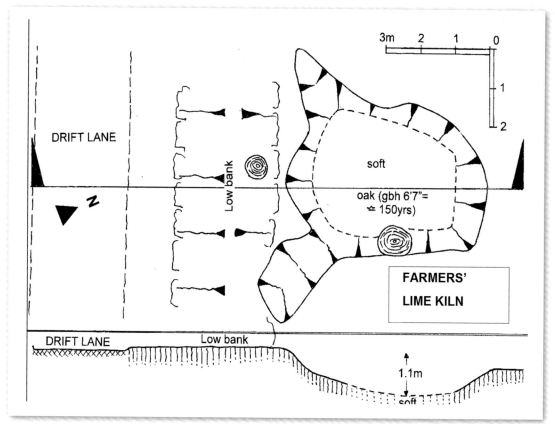

Figure 97. Survey of a Farmers' Lime Kiln.

Now some of the multitude of **smaller man-made holes**.

Farmers' Limekilns are a fairly common accompaniment to chalk quarries as discussed in the last chapter. To recap, they are a steep sided pit, 5 or 6m in diameter, with one or more air ducts leading to the bottom. They are always dug alongside a road or track because of the need to import large volumes of water to quench the quick lime and because lime is heavy. The vegetation growing on or near them can give a good idea of when they went out of use. The oak tree in the survey (Figure 97) is about 150 years old and could not have been there when the kiln was in use. Therefore the kiln went out of use in the mid 19th century.

Potash pits were also discussed in Chapter 5. Potash was made in shallow pits because the ash is so light that it is easily blown away. The need to turn and stir the fire dictates the shape, diameter and depth of the pit. If the pit was too wide the turning fork would not reach the ash in the centre. The pit illustrated in Figure 98 is circular and about 8 or 9m in diameter and only about half a metre deep. They went out of use in the mid 1800s and are only found in older

Figure 98. A probable potash pit in Hampstead Norreys woods.

woods. 'Lye' occurs in some wood names and may indicate woods where potash was regularly made. Ashampstead parish has 'Lye Wood' and 'Hartridge Lye Wood'.

If you come across a shallow oblong trench in a wood, about 3 metres long by 1½ wide (Figure 99), possibly with a low bank along one side, it is likely to be a *sawpit*. Again, I discussed their use and users in Chapter 5. Sawpits are a very common find in any wood more than a couple of hundred years old that contained standard trees. In fact, finding a wood totally devoid of sawpits either indicates that it was a pure coppice until World War 1 or that it is a recent planting. The pits were dug near the trees to be felled in advance of the sawyers' arrival and were supposed to be back filled when the work was finished, but this was often done without much enthusiasm.

One of the most difficult remains to find are ***charcoal hearths*** (Figure 102). We know that they must have been very common because so much charcoal was needed but they are not easy to spot. Charcoal burners seem to have preferred to build their ***pitstead*** on a slight slope – probably to ensure the site stayed reasonably dry (Figure 103). They then cut a small and carefully levelled terrace into the slope. The site had to be level because a slope across the base of the burning stack would cause a draught across the base and result in an uneven burn. The resulting little terrace can look very much like a ***rotational landslip***. Rotational landslips are very common in unstable geologies like the Lambeth

Figure 99. A typical back filled sawpit. The red bars are 1 metre long.

Beds on which so many West Berkshire woods are situated. Figure 100 shows how they occur. They always cause confusion among woodland archaeologists (including me!), particularly since it seems they were sometimes actually used by charcoal burners to lessen the task of digging the pitstead! Nothing is ever

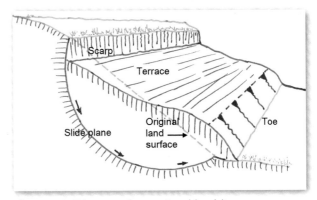

Figure 100. Diagram of a rotational landslip.

simple! The making of the charcoal necessarily left charcoal debris on the site and this is the best clue. Lots of charcoal fragments on a small terrace make it highly likely that the site was used to make charcoal. However, do not be too dogmatic because it could also be the site of a bonfire used to burn up debris resulting from more modern woodland operations.

Another piece of evidence can come from the surrounding ground flora. Once the stack of logs had been built (Figure 101) they had to be covered with turf to prevent air getting in and this turf came from the surrounding wood. Unexplained bare patches in dense bluebells may indicate the presence nearby of a charcoal kiln.

Figure 101. A charcoal stack awaiting covering. Museum of English Rural Life University of Reading.

Figure 102. Remains of a charcoal burners' hut. (This one is actually in a Chilterns wood).

The stacks had to be tended continuously day and night for at least two days. If the fire broke through the covering it would ruin the whole burn and so any holes had to be sealed with more turf (not damped with water). If the wood was green it could take even longer for the charring process to be completed. The charcoal

Figure 103. A proven charcoal site. The black lines indicate where the stack was sited.

burners made huts of various designs (Figure 104) to shelter themselves during this period. In my experience **charcoal burners' huts** are always positioned nine or ten metres southwest of the stack so that the prevailing wind will blow the fumes away from their temporary home. Having built the hut using poles from the wood and having roofed it with thatch or turfs, they often scraped the topsoil and leaf mould away from the inside to make a dry, clean floor. When the site was abandoned this construction left a very characteristic patch – see Figure 102. The fallen and rotted turf made a ring of rich soil and, with the stripped inner surface, changed the local vegetation. Sometimes a ring of stones was used to stiffen the structure.

Figure 104. Charcoal burners and their hut. Museum of English Rural Life University of Reading.

The geology of West Berkshire makes many places very suitable for **brick making**. Few if any bricks were made in England between the Roman Period and the 14th century. Roman bricks and tiles come in many shapes and sizes and look very professionally made and modern. It is best to visit a museum with a Roman Collection to see them 'in the flesh' because some Roman roof tiles can look like 19th century field drains[63].

To make a brick you need more than just clay – particularly if that clay is acidic. You need chalk or lime to counter the acid, sand to temper the clay and fuel to heat the kiln. The Lambeth Group that caps many of our hills contains the sands and clays, and the chalk is not far below them. The hilltop coppices provided an inexhaustible supply of fuel if carefully cut in rotation. A careful examination of the superb, late 19th century, First Edition of the Ordnance Survey Six inches to the Mile series of maps will reveal many 'brick and tile works' sites perched on the edge of ridges.

The earliest 'kilns' were simply clamps of clay blocks stacked in an open way with the gaps between them filled with wood fuel. The clamp was then covered

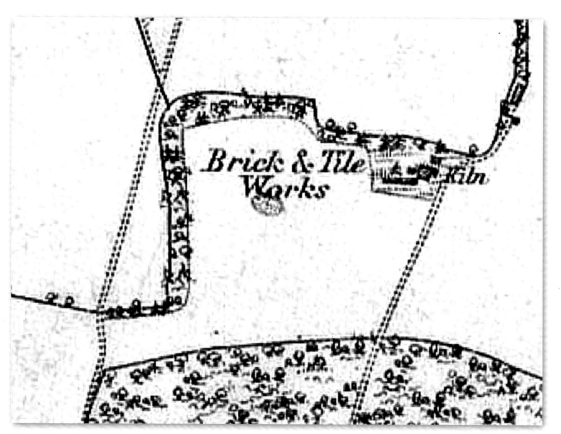

Figure 105. A typical First Edition site.

[63] Reading Museum, www.readingmuseum.org.uk has the Silchester Gallery with many examples. Newbury Museum museum@westberks.gov.uk (bricks and tiles may not be on display and an appointment may be necessary to see samples).

with more fuel and fired as a huge bonfire. The heat was very poorly distributed. It was extremely hot in the ducts and in the centre of the clamp – sometimes hot enough to distort the bricks – whereas the outside of the clamp was barely hot enough to fire the clay. If you find thin distorted bricks without a frog and varying in thickness you have probably found an early brickworks. Later on, 'Scotch kilns' were built to get around these problems. These were simply a rectangle of brick walls, many bricks thick and built without mortar, with the top left open. The walls were held together with chains and iron straps. A narrow gap was left in one side to allow the clay blocks to be stacked inside the kiln in the same way that they were stacked in a clamp. The gap was then blocked and the kiln fired. The wall contained more of the heat and ensured a more even temperature and therefore fewer spoiled bricks.

Scotch kilns were in use until 1939 when they were closed by the blackout regulations at the start of World War 2. The bright light of a firing would have attracted the attention of the Luftwaffe.

Figure 106. A Scotch Kiln.

Figure 107. The ruins of a Scotch Kiln closed in 1939. The photo was taken in 1995. Nature is taking over.

Figure 108. House foundations.

Figure 109. Well.

We now come to remains from the modern era – such as **house foundations**, **wells**, **mortared brick walls** etc (Figures 108, 109) – which most people will recognise without my help.

However, there is a class of structure with which many people may not be familiar and that is **World War 2 military structures**. West Berkshire is within a day's drive from the south coast ports and during World War 2 many of our woods were used to conceal military activities during the build-up to the invasion of Normandy (D Day). Other woods have grown up over abandoned airfields and their multitude of huts and workshops and specialist buildings. It would be impracticable to illustrate and describe all of these and so I propose only to show some of the more typical kinds.

Immediately before the invasion troops were moved from the training areas to sites that had been prepared for them in woods nearer to the coast. The men lived under canvas among the trees but temporary cookhouses and ablution blocks had been prepared in advance. The surface structures were removed

World War 2 remains

Figure 110. A temporary hut base.

Are there any of these on your land?

Figure 111. A 4m deep brick lined cistern – only covered with a rotting metal cover.

after the war leaving the **concrete bases <u>and the associated deep soak-away</u>** **<u>pits</u>**. These are now hazardous as their flimsy manhole covers have rusted away. If you know that your wood was used in this way it is well worth searching for these structures and recording them so that the wood owner can make them safe. Recently a lost dog was found at the bottom of a soak-away pit along with the remains of several deer that had died lingering deaths. Just think – they might have been children!

Other hazardous structures are **pillbox gun positions** and underground **air raid shelters**. These are now collapsing but are still fatally attractive to young – and not so young – people.

Many structures are, of course, still robust. The rectangular earth embankments used as **munition stores** are going the same way as hillforts and Roman marching camps and pose little threat to anyone.

Disused railways exist in some woods. There were very many minor branch lines and some industries built their own railways to extract minerals from quarries etc. They are usually very obvious and will be shown on early 20th century maps. Many lines were closed when the networks were rationalised between 1950 and 1970 (the Beeching Axe). Nature is taking over and in a few years time it will be difficult to distinguish between a Prehistoric ranch boundary and a late 19th century railway embankment!

Figure 112. An air raid shelter, collapsing under the weight of trees.

Figure 113. An RAF munitions store.

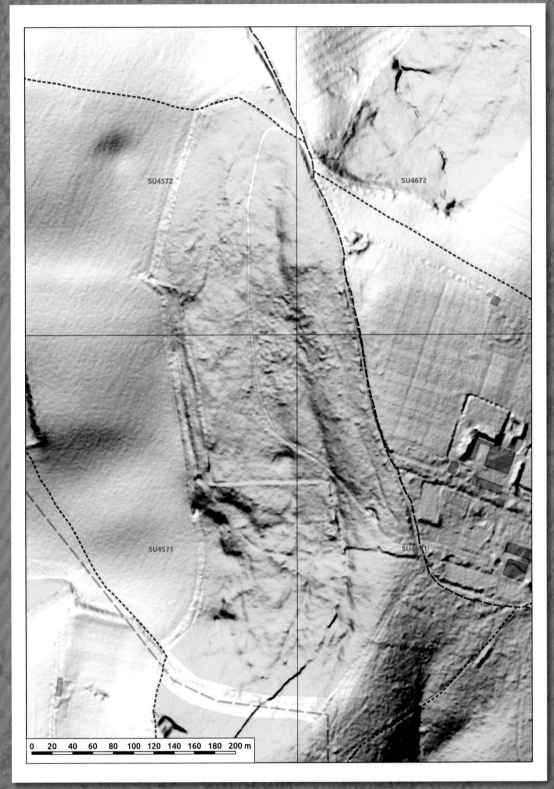

SU4572
SU4672
SU4571
SU4571

0 20 40 60 80 100 120 140 160 180 200 m

Figure 114. A LiDAR image of a wood showing ancient brick working in the south, linear ditches, geological terraces, quarry pits and other features.

N

100 metres

2

Hazel cop

4

Conifers

wetland

Chapter 7

How to REALLY get to know a wood.

Woods are wonderful places. They are full of wonders and Ancient Woods have the most. Woods are a totally different community from the outside world. Their horizons are closer, their populations completely different. No matter how long you spend in an old wood you will never learn everything about it.

Clear felled

6   BS

Hazel coppice

7 8

You can know a wood on many different levels – much as you can know another person. They can be a casual acquaintance or a deeply loved and respected companion, but you will never know everything about them. There will always be some secret. This may attract or repel you but, to me, it makes them fascinating.

At the most casual level you may drive past a wood, morning and evening, and see it in every season. It may pass simply as a green blur or you may have favourite vistas – a low autumn sun shining on a particular beech tree – but you may not be intrigued enough to stop and explore. On the other hand you may spend time in Record Offices looking for early maps, your winter leisure roaming the wood GPS in hand recording the pits, banks and hollows and your spring Sundays recording the flowers. But in between there are many levels of involvement and I will use this chapter to sketch out a few.

But first, if you do not own the wood yourself, get permission to wander from the people who do!

Remember the mantrap. You will not tread on one of these but owners still consider their woods as private and gamekeepers spend a lot of time and effort rearing their birds. Neither takes kindly to finding strangers roaming in their woods and your explorations are likely to be firmly terminated before you have even started. On the other hand, if you establish courteous and friendly relations with them and comply with any restrictions they may impose, you are likely to gather a lot of information about the wood from them that you would be unlikely to get anywhere else.

Perhaps the most **superficial level** of involvement which we may call **Level One**, is simply going for a stroll along a Public Right of Way through the wood. You can learn a lot even from this if you look and wonder, particularly if the path is an old road. What trees are growing? Are they huge and ancient or slim and in straight lines?. Are there any of the Ancient Woodland Indicator Species amongst the flowers and is one area richer than another? Are there patches of dense bluebells or areas swamped in dog's mercury? What about the boundary? Is it marked with a bank? Is the ditch on the outside to keep things out, or on the inside to keep things in? Simply noting these as you stroll along will give you a good idea whether the wood has been here for a long time – possibly centuries – or is a fairly recent plantation.

Beware! This sort of casual consumption can lead to addiction!

Level Two might take you to your computer to browse for old maps of the area. **John Rocque's Survey of Berkshire** is the oldest general map and the **First Edition of the Ordnance Survey 6 inches : 1 mile** the best. They both cover the whole of Old Berkshire.

Almost all parishes have **Tithe Awards**. These were made in the 1840s when the Tithe – the landowner's payment to the Church – was changed from payment in kind to payment in cash. They are in two parts – a very detailed Map of the parish surveyed extremely accurately and an Award document listing the owner and the tenant's name for each patch of land and giving a general description of its use. Both of these are held in the Berkshire Record Office in Reading[64] and can be freely examined. You should make an appointment before you go and, if it is your first visit, take some form of identification with you that will enable you to be issued with a Reader's Ticket.

Park Wood and Down Wood at Hampstead Norreys

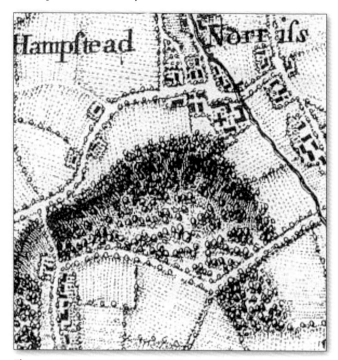

Figure 115. Rocque's Survey 1761.

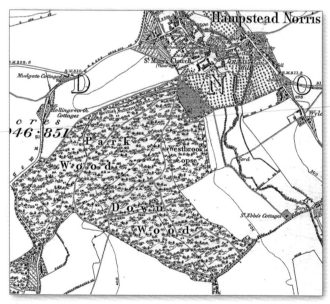

Figure 116. First Edition OS of the same wood 1877.

[64] Berkshire Record Office. 01189 375132 www.berkshirerecordoffice.org.uk

While you are there it would be well worth consulting one of the archivists – they are very knowledgeable and helpful people. With their help, look through their catalogues to see if they hold other records of your wood. Many parishes and landowners have deposited their older archives with the Record Office.

House's Farm

No.1 House Barton & Acre Orchard

				£	s	d
9	Elms	391 Feet	at 2/-	39	2	0
2	Walnuts	34 Feet	at 4/-	6	16	0
1	Oak	35 Feet	at 5/-	8	15	0
13	Ash & Elm Saplings & 3 Pollards			4	17	0
			value	159	10	0

Figure 117. A transcribed extract from a survey of woods made in 1820.

Back in your wood you can compare the modern wood with the wood on the old maps. Has it expanded or shrunk? Does the ground flora illustrate the changes?

A practical example may help. As can be seen in Figure 118 there appears to have been two phases of expansion at Costrills Copse. The first expansion was into the NW corner where tree symbols are shown but where there are no bluebells. This must have occurred before 1910 when the base map was published. The second expansion was onto the heathland and field along the eastern edge at some date after 1910. My survey was carried out in 2004. In the intervening

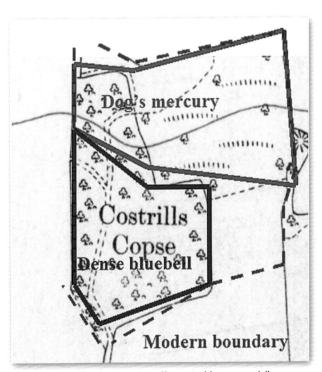

Figure 118. Wood expansion illustrated by ground flora.

Figure 119. Dog's mercury.

Figure 120. A bluebell glade.

94 years the bluebells had not spread significantly from the original wood in the SW corner thus adding support for Oliver Rackham's assertion that in East Anglia they spread at only about a metre per hundred years.

You might consider spending some sunny spring days sketching in the areas of bluebells and dog's mercury in your wood. You don't need to be a botanist to do this, nor do you need expensive survey equipment. There are many worse things to do than strolling around a wood mapping bluebells!

Before the undergrowth gets too high it would be interesting to record the boundary banks and any internal banks. It is very likely that these will be already shown as a solid line on your copy of the First Edition OS map. But add the ditch. I personally use Oliver Rackham's symbols because I find them clear and adaptable.

||||||||||||||||||||||||||||| **is a bank**

_____ **is a ditch**

By varying the length and density of the bank symbol lines you can indicate the size of the bank. A wide dense strip indicates a large bank and widely spaced light lines a fainter bank. Similarly a wide red line indicates a wide deep ditch and a fine one a modest ditch.

If there are any structures or pits in the wood, a photograph and a cross on your map will be an adequate record. It is a good idea to include a companion or your notepad or something similar in the photograph to give an idea of scale.

On another visit you might record a sample of the trees and the understorey. Again, you do not need to be a botanist to recognise the trees and shrubs you are likely to find in a West Berkshire wood and a simple tree recognition book will be all that you need. Measure the girth of a few of the largest. I will explain later how to estimate their age using their girth.

By high summer you will have made a very respectable record of your wood and you can put the map away until the winter. High summer is no time to survey a wood.

By now, even if you don't own the wood, it will be becoming very much <u>your</u> wood in the sense that someone you see regularly and have shared time with is <u>your</u> friend. And the friendship will grow and deepen the more time you share together but you will <u>never</u> know everything!

Figure 121. A deciduous wood in summer. All historical and archaeological features invisible.

Figure 122. A coniferous wood in summer. Surveying possible.

And now we come to the serious stuff! **Level Three**. Please skip this section unless you seriously want to make a **detailed study of the wood**. As with any serious study, a detailed survey takes **commitment, planning and equipment**.

Starting with the **commitment**. A detailed survey is not something that can be done whilst walking the dog, nor can it be done in company with someone lacking the same commitment.

Although coniferous woods and beech woods are generally free of bracken, nettles and brambles and can be surveyed in summer, the only season when minor archaeological features are visible in a deciduous wood is winter, and late winter at that, when frost, rain and gales have flattened the undergrowth. Winter is also the shooting season and many West Berkshire woods are maintained for pheasant shooting. The last shooting day is 1st February. This coincides nicely with minimum undergrowth and lengthening days and so is a good time to start your surveying.

And now the *planning*.

It may seem obvious, but first check that a survey does not already exist for your wood. The best source of information is the West Berkshire Historic Environment Record (HER)[65]. This is held in the West Berkshire Planning Department and comprises a map based electronic record of all reported archaeological and historic sites in West Berkshire. The organisation is short staffed and very busy but very helpful to researchers. Be sure to lodge a copy of your research with it to help build up the knowledge base.

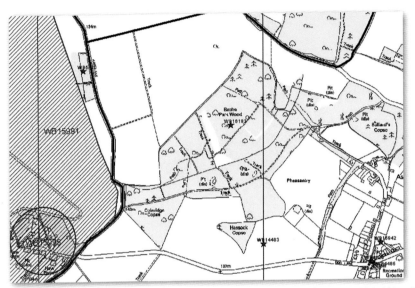

Figure 123. An extract from a HER record map. Compare with Figure 126. West Berkshire Council 2006.

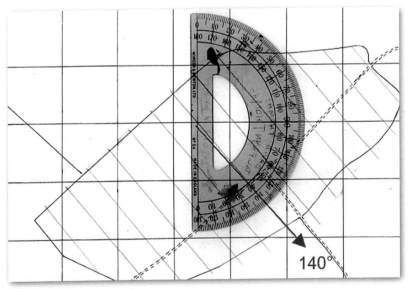

Figure 124. The survey planning map.

[65] www.westberks.gov.uk/HER

The usual method of mapping archaeology in a wood is the 'walk through'. This equates to the Level One superficial level described above and, although it is very pleasant, it cannot possibly produce a detailed survey. For a detailed result the wood has to be <u>searched</u> and the route of the search must be recorded because it is almost as important to know where you have <u>not been</u> as to know where you <u>have been</u>. Efficient searches of any kind have to be planned taking into consideration the terrain, the density of the wood and the visibility within it. Draw your search lines on a map and work out the compass direction in which they run. In the diagram (Figure 124) the lines run 140° on the way out and 320° on the way back. It is unlikely that the wood will let you stick to the lines, even in winter, but the plan provides a framework that, if followed, would give you a good chance of seeing most – if not all – of the archaeological features in the wood.

Equipment should be kept to a minimum. Part of the fun is making one piece of kit do more than one job. I have seen surveyors going into woods laden like First World War infantrymen – even carrying bundles of surveyors' red and white poles! Why take a stick into a wood?

You need

- A map to find your way to the start of your search lines.

- A magnetic compass to give you the general direction of the line you intend to follow. Remember that GPS compasses only work when you are moving, although some units have a built-in magnetic compass.

- Some way of finding your position in the wood which you can transfer to your map and which you can also use to position any feature you may find. In a small wood simply pacing along a compass bearing may

Figure 125. Survey equipment.

be adequate as long as you first check the length of your pace by walking along a length measured with a tape. If the expenditure is justified, buy a hand held GPS of the type used for orienteering and geocaching, but make sure that it has a sensitive antenna that will allow it to produce a position under tree canopies. You may already have a phone that will do the job, but surveying woods can be rough and I personally use kit designed for the purpose. At the moment (2016) an adequate GPS costs about £80. There are vast numbers of software packages to allow you to load your search grid onto the instrument, to record your actual route, the positions of features, photograph positions and later to download them onto your computer for plan production. These all change by the day and so it is pointless trying to go into details here. If computers are not your thing, it is perfectly adequate to read your grid references off the GPS and record them on your field sheet for later plotting with a scale and pencil on a paper map.

- A camera to photograph features.
- A 15m tape to take dimensions of larger features and a pocket tape for smaller ones.
- A clipboard to hold your map and recording sheet.
- A pole which can double as a marker, a photographic scale, walking stick and measuring stick for simple measurements.
- A flask of beverage of your choice and a sustaining snack.
- And most importantly a good pair of boots and patience.

Survey technique. This may sound complex but isn't and is really very logical. It is thorough and reasonably quick.

- Find your way to the start of your first line.
- Observe the planned direction using your compass and pick out a mark to walk towards.
- Walk along the line scanning the wood on either side. After (say) 30 paces, stop, put your marker pole into the ground, record its position and explore around it. Make sure the pole has a bright flag of some sort; it is very easy to lose a brown stick in a brown wood!
- Record the position and measurements of any features found and photograph as necessary.
- Return to your marker pole and carry on along the line stopping and searching as necessary.

- When an area is impenetrable go around it recording your route, note that it has not been examined and try to return to the line beyond the dense area before resuming the search.

- At the far edge of the wood, pause for a cup from your flask – you will have earned it – move to the start of the next line and repeat the procedure.

Woodland survey is tiring because you must concentrate on several different things at once – navigating, looking and recording. Keep your visits fairly short to avoid exhaustion. I find it best done alone to remove the temptation to chat!

Mapping and recording the result.

- It is wise to make a preliminary plot of your day's work as soon as possible at the end of each day while the site is still fresh in your memory.

- Do not re-write field sheets – always keep the originals. Mud and coffee stains are honourable scars.

- In your written summary, keep descriptions of features and your interpretation of them separate because you may be wrong. *Rectangular shallow pit 2.5m x 3.5m – probable sawpit* is better than *Sawpit 2.5m x 3.5m*.

- When the survey is complete produce a hard copy report as well as a digital one. There is going to be a Dark Ages in our history due to digital data being lost or becoming unreadable by future machines as systems change.

- Provide a copy to the HER.

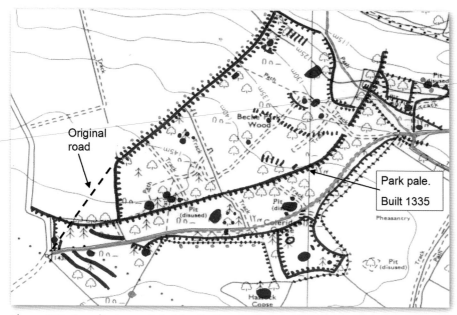

Figure 126. A preliminary plot of the findings in the wood shown in Figure 123.

Using the trees, understorey and ground flora to inform the survey.

The woodland archaeologist should make simultaneous use of as many lines of inquiry as possible. An argument involving vegetation and earthworks is generally more convincing than one based on vegetation alone. Investigators who confine themselves to written evidence sooner or later run into the Scylla of pseudo-history; those confined to field evidence are caught by the Charybdis of circular argument. Even in the best-documented wood, there is always something more to be learned from fieldwork.

Oliver Rackham[66]

It is usual for boundary banks to have trees and coppice stools growing on them. On the boundary of an Ancient Wood the coppice stools may be huge and much older than the neighbouring standard trees – no matter how large. The stool in Figure 127 is one of very many in an area largely devoid of Ancient Trees. Logically, if the stool is 750 years old, the bank it is standing on must be at least 750 years old and may be much older. It stands amid very dense bluebells on the boundary bank around Franklin's Copse near Frilsham. A franklin was a man who held his land freely without owing labour services to the lord of the manor and two franklins are recorded in Domesday Book for the Manor of Frilsham.

It is impossible to calculate the age of any tree – standard or coppice stool – without cutting it down or extracting a core and counting the rings. The best that can be achieved is an <u>estimate</u>, and in many cases only a <u>guestimate</u>. Nevertheless, intelligently used, this can add to the story of your wood. Oliver Rackham provides a rule-of-thumb for estimating the age of coppice stools[67]. You measure the diameter of the stool in two or three directions and take the average. For oak, lime, hazel and ash allow 0.3m (1 foot) for each century. Field maple grows a little faster. Sweet chestnut and sycamore probably grow twice as fast. Every time the poles were harvested from the stool it almost stopped growing and the annual rings will be very narrow. The stool has to wait for the canopy to recover before starting to grow normally again. I have christened this **Coppice Shock**. As a result a stool of a given size will be older than a standard tree of the same size. Figure 128 explains this.

Stools within the wood show what the wood was being used for when they were established. However there may have been other trees before them. Trees change with the market for wood and timber. When sheep need penning, hazel and ash coppice will be grown. When ships are needed the coppice may

---

[66] Rackham O.(1990) *Trees and Woodland in the British Landscape.* 107

[67] Rackham O. (2006) *Woodlands* 248

Figure 127. Ash stool on a coppice bank. 2.2m average diameter. Possibly 750 years old.

be converted to grow oak standards.

Standard or Maiden Trees are what most people would call trees – tall straight pillars of wood with branches near the top. When they are large enough to serve a particular purpose they are felled and removed. It is unusual to find very old standards in a wood because they were regularly harvested and didn't have the chance to grow old.

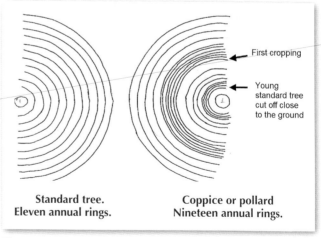

First cropping

Young standard tree cut off close to the ground

Standard tree.
Eleven annual rings.

Coppice or pollard
Nineteen annual rings.

Figure 128. Coppice shock.

Estimating the age of standard trees is fraught with danger. Two identical trees established at the same time can be completely different in size after a century or so if one had more light, water and shelter than the other. However, it can be useful to have some idea of the ages of the trees in a wood and, as usual, there are two ways of doing it – the crude approximation using the Aging Diagram (Figure 129) and the statistically better way using John White's detailed observations published on the Forestry Commission website.

www.forestry.gov.uk/pdf/fcin12.pdf/$file/fcin12.pdf

For both methods first measure the tree's girth (circumference) at about 1.5m above the ground and apply it to the curve. Bear in mind that this curve is little better than a rule-of-thumb based on my own measurements and ring counts, polished with older published data. It will give an indication of age for oak, ash and beech standard trees growing in reasonably open conditions. If the tree is a pollard add another 30%.

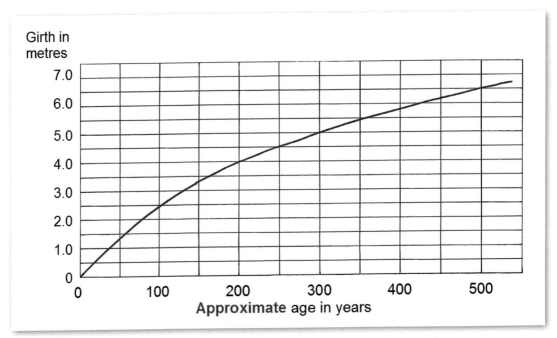

Figure 129. Tree aging curve.

But beware of ancient yews! Ancient yews develop in ways different from other trees and yew aging is very contentious and often strays into the realms of fantasy. Use John White's methods for these.

As with most things in woodland archaeology, there are complications. Sometimes a standard tree's stump was allowed to shoot to form a coppice stool and was cropped for a few cycles. At a later date a single strong stem might be allowed to grow and become a standard tree. This may then have been cut off at about two metres to form a pollard. Aging such a tree is extremely difficult. I think the sweet chestnut in Figure 1 on page VIII may have developed in this way.

Pollards are rare in woods although they may occur on the boundary bank where they would not have suffered if the field next to the wood was grazed. Finding them in a wood probably indicates that the wood was a Common before becoming covered with trees. Pollards are subject the same irregular growth patterns as coppice stools. Their age can be estimated from Figure 129 by adding 30% to the age of a standard tree of the same girth.

Understorey trees such as birch, cherry, field maple, thorn and sycamore probably invaded when serious management ceased, although some had special uses. For instance, birch was used for brooms and sycamore for dairy implements. In a very old wood they may have survived from wood pasture days and been tolerated, but this was more likely to happen on a Common. Occasionally you may find them forming an old hedge buried in the wood. The Record Office's old maps may allow you to identify their original purpose.

Figure 130. An ancient layered hedge buried in a wood giving evidence for land use.

Few bluebells

Dense bluebells

Figure 131. An ancient abandoned field highlighted by dense dog's mercury.

Mapping ground flora is very important to the study of a wood but must be used with care and combined with consideration of the effects of the local soils.

As explained earlier (Chapter 6), certain plants are recognised as indicators of Ancient Woodland. These are generally those with poor seed dispersal mechanisms that once destroyed rarely return. Woodland plants have to flower and set seed before the tree canopy closes and cuts off the light so this part of the survey will have to be done in early spring – a very pleasurable task.

Unless you are an accomplished botanist it is probably better to concentrate on the more obvious species such as bluebells, wood anemones, wood melick and ransoms. Dog's mercury in small quantities is considered a sign of Ancient Woodland, but when it occurs in dense mats it becomes a sign of anciently disturbed land. This is particularly true in some of West Berkshire's woods on acid soils like the Lambeth Group where they overlie chalk. In this case, if an area of Ancient Woodland Indicators had been cleared to make a field, the acid soil would have had to have its pH raised by the application of chalk before anything would grow. If subsequently the cleared land was abandoned or planted as coppice, dog's mercury – which prospers on calcareous soils – would quickly invade and form a mat that would inhibit the introduction of other species. This is well illustrated in Figure 131 where the cleared area has been planted with hazel coppice. It was possible to identify the field on the local Tithe Award map. However, if the whole wood had been on calcareous soils the effect would not be so obvious. Small open patches amongst bluebells etc may be the result of turf stripping to cover charcoal kilns.

Figure 132 illustrates the use of ground flora mapping to provide possible interpretations of the history of a wood.

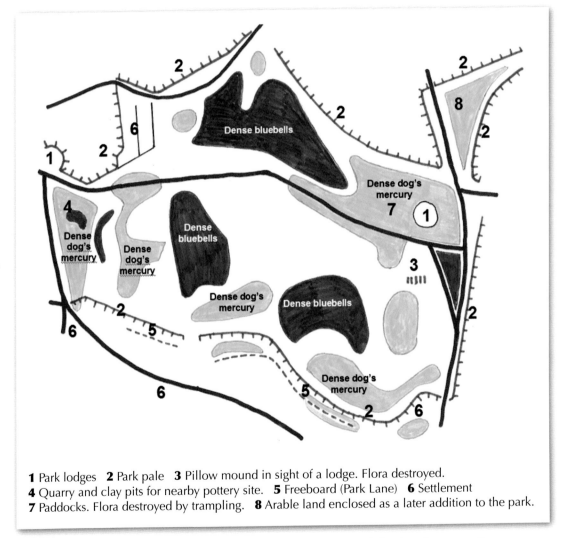

1 Park lodges   **2** Park pale   **3** Pillow mound in sight of a lodge. Flora destroyed.
4 Quarry and clay pits for nearby pottery site.   **5** Freeboard (Park Lane)   **6** Settlement
7 Paddocks. Flora destroyed by trampling.   **8** Arable land enclosed as a later addition to the park.

Figure 132. A simplified flora distribution diagram of part of a deer park that later became a Common.

A possible explanation of this diagram might be:

The quarrying and clay digging at (**4**) destroyed the bluebells and brought chalk to the surface thus encouraging dog's mercury.

The eastern lodge was positioned at (**1**) overlooking the pillow mound (**3**) and roads and entrances to the deer park. The western lodge overlooked an artificial pond (not shown).

The use of (**7**) as paddocks for the parker destroyed the woodland plants and introduced the cowslips and other grassland plants.

The positioning of the small settlements at (**6**) encouraged access through the pale when the area reverted to being a Common. Localised use removed the woodland flora.

The dense bluebell areas survived in remoter areas and where hazel coppicing took place.

It is quite possible that all of this is wrong.

This is something for the computer expert but produces remarkable results if you can handle it. BUT, like all 'black box' techniques, results should be ground truthed by someone in a pair of muddy boots before being accepted as a reliable description of a landscape!

The name LiDAR has caused much confusion. It actually derives from Light Radar[68] and refers to scanning any remote surface with a laser beam. For our purposes it means *airborne laser scanning*. An aircraft fitted with a scanner flies over the survey area continuously fixing its position in all three dimensions using the Global Positioning System (GPS). The scanner sends pulses of light against the surface and times the delay between sending and receiving the reflected light. It then uses the delay to calculate the range of the point on the surface from the aircraft. Highly sensitive gyroscopes provide the direction of the beam. By combining the range with the direction and the GPS position the position of the illuminated point on the surface is computed and becomes part of a 3D point cloud from which a digital terrain model (DTM) can be produced. The resolution of the model depends on the rate of scanning and the altitude and speed of the aircraft.

A gridded digital terrain model is produced from the DTM and provides the coordinates for a regular pattern of points as National Grid values for Eastings and Northings and altitudes above Ordnance Datum.

The next stage is the production of a terrain-shaded relief map of the area. The altitudes are hugely exaggerated to emphasise small differences in altitude and the model is 'lit' from different directions to create 'shadows' which show even small differences in altitude very clearly. Sometimes these features are so small that, although obvious on the model, they are invisible on the ground. Whilst helping to ground truth a LiDAR survey of Savernake we were unable to see the low banks of a field system that was obvious on the model.

The usefulness of the model depends on the terrain it is recording. For puposes of searching woodland for archaeological features the smaller the resolution the better. The laser light penetrates some types of woodland better than others. A reasonably open deciduous wood will allow good penetration and thus a useful model. Dense conifers are difficult to penetrate and the resulting model should be used with caution and thoroughly ground truthed.

The Environment Agency has surveyed most of England and Wales as part of its Flood Risk Mapping programme and has made the data freely available to the public[69]. The resolutions vary depending on the location and the Environment

---

[68] https://en.wikipedia.org/wiki/Lidar

[69] http://environment.data.gov.uk/ds/survey

Agency's requirements for the data. The available resolutions are 0.5m, 1.0m, and 2.0m and the areas of these are shown on the Agency's website. The image at the start of this chapter (Figure 114) was derived from the 1.0m dataset.

The beauty of a terrain-shaded relief map is that it can be explored in detail by enlarging sections, by altering the degree of altitude exaggeration and by illuminating it from different directions. It can also provide views and fly-overs and can be used to calculate volumes of quarries etc.

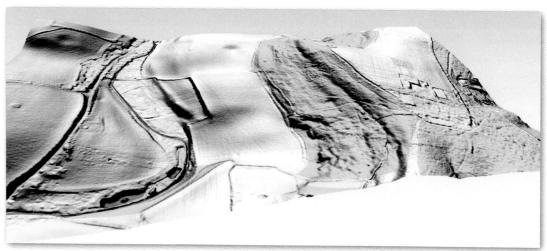

Figure 133. An oblique view along a wood clearly showing the disturbed area which ground truthing has shown to be caused by ancient brick working. Environment Agency Open Data.

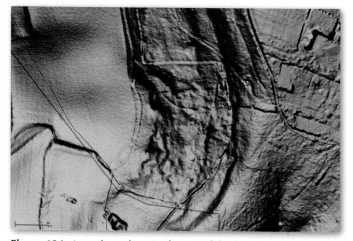

Figure 134. An enlarged vertical view of the brick workings. This degree of detail would have taken many days to produce using ground survey techniques. Environment Agency Open Data.

Figure 135. Beeches on an ancient boundary.

Chapter 8

Conclusion.

I hope a reader who has got this far in my book now agrees with me that anyone who lives near a wood in West Berkshire is blessed and that anyone who has access to an Ancient Wood is doubly blessed!

Writing this book has been a stimulating exercise. A lot of the research I have carried out over the years has been driven by the need to supply information about woods and the countryside demanded by people who have attended my talks and joined me on walks. These were first organised by the Pang, Kennet and Lambourn Valleys Project and later by the West Berkshire Countryside Society. Putting the information on paper has brought back the pleasure of remembered walks and talks and the intelligent, knowledgeable and enquiring people I met.

But beware! 'From those to whom much has been granted, much can be expected'. It is all very well studying a wood and growing to love it but surely this incurs a degree of responsibility – even if you do not own the wood? Surely you have a duty of care – as you would for a friend. If the wood is yours, treat it with respect so that future generations – perhaps your own descendants – can derive the same satisfaction from it that you have. If the wood is not yours the duty of care should at least extend to sharing your findings with the owner, who by now may well be your friend, and gently influencing his or her management of the wood to preserve its interest.

I wish you every success in your research – whichever level you choose – and I hope you derive as much life enhancing pleasure and satisfaction from your studies as I have derived from mine.

FIGURES

Arnold J.	1968	*The Shell Book of Country Crafts*	Shell
Astill G, Grant A. (Eds.)	1988	*The Countryside of Medieval England*	Blackwell
Blandford PW	1974	*Country Craft Tools*	David & Charles
Clottes J.	2008	*Cave Art*	Phaidon
Defoe D.	1724–6 1986	*A Tour Through the Whole Island of Great Britain*	Penguin Classics
Dyer C.	2007	*The Self-contained Village?*	Hertfordshire Press
Eckwall E. (Ed.)	1974	*The Concise Dictionary of English Place-names. 4th Edition*	Oxford
Edlin H.L.	1973	*The Woodland Crafts of Britain*	David & Charles
Evans G.E	1975	*The Environment of Early Man in the British Isles*	Book Club Associates
Hoskins W.G	1977	*The Making of the English Landscape*	Pelican
Mileson S.A	2009	*Parks in Medieval England*	Oxford
Morris J. (Ed.)	1979	*History from the Sources. Domesday Book. Berkshire*	Phillimore
O'Connor T, Sykes N (Eds.)	2010	*Extinctions and Invasions. A Social History of British Fauna*	Windgather
Peterken G.F.	1996	*Natural Woodland. Ecology and conservation in northern temperate regions*	Cambridge
Rackham O.	1983	*Trees and Woodland in the British Landscape*	Dent
Rackham O.	1986	*The History of the Countryside*	Phoenix
Rackham O.	2003	*Ancient Woodland. Its history, vegetation and uses in England*	Castlepoint
Rackham O.	2006	*Woodlands*	Collins
Roberts N.	1998	*The Holocene. An Environmental History*	Blackwell
Rotherham I.D. (Ed.)	2013	*Cultural Severance and the Environment*	Springer
Sturt G	1993	*The Wheelwright's Shop*	Cambridge
Tusser T.	1559 reprint 1984	*Five hundred points of good husbandry*	Oxford University Press
Vera F.W.M	2004	*Grazing Ecology and Forest History*	CABI
Williamson T.	2003	*Shaping Medieval Landscapes*	Windgather
Williamson T.	2006	*The Archaeology of Rabbit Warrens*	Shire
Williamson T.	2010	*The Origins of Hertfordshire*	Hertfordshire Publications

INDEX

INDEX